Messages from readers

This is a profoundly moving book . . . searingly honest, uplifting, interesting and ultimately hopeful. It does not seek to offer simple solutions or unrealistic expectations, but it gives the best portrait I have read of the cruel disease that is anorexia.

K. Waldegrave

Perfect is beautifully written and very moving. I am certain that this book will help many people affected by anorexia but will also touch a far greater audience than just those who have a connection to this illness. Well done Emily on an absolutely wonderful book.

Maggi x

I love this book . . . A few people I know have been affected by this cancer of the soul, and I wanted to read a real person's story of how they coped. I found it. It's amazing . . . You truly are an inspiration.

Becky xxx

Hi Emily,
I am currently in recovery stage and am reading your book at the moment and cannot tell you how much it is helping me . . . thank you so much for writing about your experiences and helping us all.

Sam x

I have just finished reading your book, and I admire your courage . . . your book brought a glimmer of hope, that maybe one day things will somehow change, and I'll reach out and grab that glimmer.

All the best,
Louise x

Emily,
Your raw honesty brought me to tears more than once – I felt like I was standing beside you through the whole experience. I just wanted to say well done but more importantly – thank you.

Lots of love,
Mia

I have just finished your book and thought it was absolutely amazing. I have anorexia and am just beginning the recovery stage . . . your book has inspired me . . . it has really made me see and think into what my family have gone through and how this disease has affected them too. Thank you.

Much love,
Kristen xo

Dear Emily,

[*Perfect*] is beautifully written . . . As a clinician, I have had some direct experience of the problem: every fact and thought I could remember from my cases was retrieved in your narrative, which, it seems to me, could stand as a clinical lesson on anorexia . . . [My] empathy and admiration for the fine person you are.

With best wishes,
Ele Ferrannini, MD, Professor of Medicine

A brave and inspiring story by a brave and inspiring person.

Rose xxx

Dear Emily,

I was both fascinated and saddened by your story. I knew nothing about anorexia until now, but as the mum of two girls it is something I've thought about . . . What I found so remarkable was the way in which you were so lucid, so clearly able to understand what was happening to you while it was going on. I am sure it must be really inspirational to other young women struggling with similar issues – from someone who understands, doesn't judge and who survived!

From a mother

I am a counsellor and *Perfect* is one of the most informative and totally honest books on anorexia that I have read. This book does not back away from reality, and through that reality there is hope for all anorexics. If you are anorexic read this book, if you are a parent or sibling of an anorexic read this book.

Mrs. Kerry D. Beck

Emily. I could not put this book down. Each word is from experience and the heart ... I think even those not connected to the illness in any sense would find your book well worth reading. You should be very proud of yourself – not just for your book. Thank you.

Emma x

To be in touch with Emily, please visit:
www.emilyhalban.wordpress.com

Perfect

anorexia
& me

Emily Halban

Vermilion
LONDON

3 5 7 9 10 8 6 4 2

Published in 2008 by Vermilion, an imprint of Ebury Publishing
This edition published by Vermilion in 2009

Ebury Publishing is a Random House Group company

The Random House Group Limited Reg. No. 954009

Addresses for companies within the Random House Group can be found at
www.rbooks.co.uk

A CIP catalogue record for this book is available from the British Library

Mixed Sources
Product group from well-managed
forests and other controlled sources
www.fsc.org Cert no. TT-COC-2139
© 1996 Forest Stewardship Council

The Random House Group Limited supports The Forest Stewardship
Council (FSC), the leading international forest certification organisation.
All our titles that are printed on Greenpeace approved FSC certified paper
carry the FSC logo. Our paper procurement policy can be found at
www.rbooks.co.uk/environment

Printed in the UK by CPI Cox & Wyman, Reading, RG1 8EX

ISBN 9780091917494

Copies are available at special rates for bulk orders. Contact the sales
development team on 020 7840 8487 for more information.

To buy books by your favourite authors and register for offers, visit
www.rbooks.co.uk

Acknowledgements

For lack of a better way to express, in various degrees and with varying words, my gratitude, I will have to resort to a simple, sweeping, thank you:

To maman and to my daddy: for your presence, your support, your gentle encouragement, your unwavering devotion. For believing in me when I no longer would, and for trusting me when I no longer could. Thank you, over and over again, never enough. To Patrick: for knowing me, for hearing me, for being there, always, no matter what. To Amanda: for sistering like a mother, and mothering like a sister, and for being an inspirational mummy, too. To Sam: I pause. Nothing I say will ever express how appreciative I am of the hand you rest on my shoulder. No language will ever sufficiently tell of the love that keeps my heart beating, for you. You are all that is good in me, and you make me want to better myself. To Sue: in memoriam. To Lally, my grandmother: for your warmth, your attentiveness, your affection. *Ton ange t'aime fort.* To my friends, every one of you: for

5

drawing laughter out of a tear. To Olivia: 'til Oxford – and beyond. To Aude and Kimmins: for a happy childhood reminding me, all the time, of who I am. To Vanessa, ma Nouni: for caring so much, for your warmth, your smiles, your hugs. To Roxy, my little bookworm: for 'getting' me beyond anything spoken, for our giggles, our chats, for all our time shared, and so much more to come. To Isabelle: for memories. To Ellie: forever saying the right thing, forever rubbing shine on my tarnished self-esteem, forever a friend. To Katie: for knowing me so well (too well?). To Maria: for minding, for being thoughtful, for making me feel secure. To Spence, the very Best Man ever. To Meels, my darling mumsy Meels. To Alex, my Moomsy: for listening, really listening. For your softness, your happiness, your gentle ways. You are special. To Louise: for introducing me to the little girl inside, who felt so frightened and unsafe that she could only hide. To Vicki: for bringing pleasure to my plate, for bringing colour to my cheeks, for your infectious enthusiasm. To both Louise and Vicki: for teaching me through and through that it really is okay. To Penny: my sunshine in a box, for seeing brightness through the clouds. And to Imogen: for drawing this book out of me. To Caroline: for putting in the good word, over and over again. To Clare: for offering me the chance. To Miranda: for taking it to print. To Justine: for detail that made the difference. To all: for making the dream come true.

Thank You.

Prologue

I write, not because I feel that I deserve any special merit for what I have been through. I do not claim the following pages to be worthy of special attention. I feel the need to share my experience precisely because it is not *extra*-ordinary. Day after day the amount of individuals bound – or bound to be bound – by the same fate seems to escalate at a worrying scale.

Many volumes have already been written on the subject. Some stories that have been published in the past are those of lifelong destitution and hardship. When I read through such heart-rending pages, I feel guilty. I was privileged: gifted, happy, pampered, cared for and loved; my anorexia hit me just as hard. There have been self-help books, medical accounts and explanations in so far as they exist. However, when I was ill, such documents only served to guide me further into my illness. Whenever I came across a symptom I did not possess, I was quick to put it into practice too. When I studied the ways in which to put on weight, I assiduously did all I could to perform the opposite. Anorexia has a perverse way of twisting a helping hand into a forceful grip that drags the suffering patient deeper into Hell.

What I desperately looked for at the time, and still wish I could find today, were details as to what happens when one does begin to recover. After accepting that one has the illness, after seeking help, after beginning to put on weight. When I began to eat again I was so afraid the hunger would never subside. I was afraid I would start to binge permanently. My idea of a gargantuan portion may still have been another's slimming dish, but when – how – would I learn to understand what a 'normal' quantity really was? Why was I no longer able to digest certain foods for a while? Was the weight going to stop escalating at some point? How could I know if I really was totally okay? What did that feel like anyway? No one realises how difficult the last few steps actually are. No matter how well supplied with crutches and support, I was still exhausted, afraid and incredibly confused. I needed someone to tell me what recovery was like. I wanted to hear a trustworthy real-life version of what I was to expect. I wanted a 'role-model' with whom I could identify. I want my book to answer those whose questions still are not met. And I want to stress that anorexia is an *illness*. It is a cancer of the soul and it is nobody's fault. It *can* be healed.

Anorexia creeps into the family. People close to the victim often suffer just as much. They feel just as vulnerable and frightened. Very often they will manage to handle the situation as long as their loved one is still on the road to recovery. However, when the one they cared for finally does pull through, such individuals, faced with demons they managed to silence for so long, will typically spiral into similar or other forms of depression in turn.

I wish I could offer a coherent 'once upon a time'. I wish I could say exactly when it all began, where and how and why. I can trace no traumatic experience that suddenly turned my world upside down. My story is not that of a miserable childhood shattered with horrifying tales to recount. I did not drink (a lot), I did not smoke (that often); the only drug I knew of was that sweet raspberry syrup I was sometimes given as a child to help me sleep. Mine is the dreamed portrait of a perfect little girl come from a perfect family of five living in a perfect *House & Garden* home with a puppy dog and a big kitchen and an innumerable amount of perfect friends. My life was perfectly balanced and I was perfectly happy: everything was in perfect blissful, innocent and harmless control. Then control took control and I was left with no control. It took me years to work out that things didn't have to be perfect.

Perfection is a disease that wipes out all that really is

perfect in life, only to replace it with an idealistic approximation that keeps us in a constant state of dissatisfaction and disarray. Perfection was my disease; anorexia was my perfection.

1

No matter how hard I try to trace my anorexia back to a 'very beginning', I find myself turning round in circles and scraping thin air. Perhaps it was always there, looming in the distance and growing silently with time? Perhaps there was a set of events that eventually tumbled out of control and left an empty space all too ready to be filled with the bug? I don't know where to begin, but in the beginning of 'me' there was my mother, naturally, and every day my mother continues to play a central role in my life.

And so I choose to start with the day my mother lost her laugh.

I would prefer not to have to open my story with a portrait of my mother, because this will send me – and her – straight into the simplified statistics basket; the one that says that anorexia can generally always be linked back to the mother and that the mother of an anorexic child is generally domineering, heavy-handed, and that the mother must be kept away from her anorexic child in order for that child to grow, independently, without parental pressure. But in fact, that is exactly why I feel the burning need to write. To overcome those fixed ideas.

Such conveniently drawn conclusions are limited and dangerous. They offer a mould into which we all too easily melt. Because we want an explanation; we want flow charts and diagrams; we need to box, classify, and file. We have lost our ability to listen, to let things be told the way they were, the way they felt, from the heart.

I am writing from the heart. And when I think back I do believe my mother's sudden sadness played some part not so much in causing, but perhaps more in disclosing whatever it was that made me stop eating.

I was fifteen years old, and until then had only heard my mother weep once. My mother who is always so positive, so forward thinking, so strong. She loves to laugh. She loves to love. She made me laugh; she taught me love. These are gifts that have helped to pull me through my darkest days time and time again. But then, one day, she shared pain with me as well.

When I write that my mother is strong, you might read that as authoritarian or overbearing. Yet by 'strong' I mean that my mother has a very strong character and an acutely intuitive nature, particularly when it comes to sensing what is right or wrong for her children. Simply put, my mother, just like any other mother, has always wanted what was best for her children and always believed that what was best would occur. And she has always protected us from harm, in a way only mothers know how.

My parents, brother, sister and I are all very close. Mine is one of those families where we tend to be involved, to some degree, with whatever is going on in each other's daily lives. If one of us has a problem, it quickly becomes a common issue and we look to finding a way to make it okay. We are all about solutions. There is this sense we have of knowing what's best for each other, and somehow doing what's best better than anyone else; perfectly, almost.

My mother married twice which means, strictly speaking, that my siblings are 'half'. I would never consider them as such; I never have and nor will I, ever. We were all brought up together, under the same roof, and treated the same both by our mother and by my father. My parents were so careful not to highlight any difference between the three of us in fact that I grew up calling my father by his first name 'Philippe', just like everyone else did (I secretly hated it when friends asked me why I called him so and deep down I wished that I could say 'daddy' instead). Nevertheless, the reality is that we do not share the same biological father. And the reason this is important for me to add is that I have always held a fear – one I have voiced to them more than once – that my brother and sister might one day feel an attachment with each other that I cannot share; a connection that will not link back to me. Through childhood – and beyond – there has been that creeping sense of guilt for having my dad around, for being the child from a marriage without divorce.

Guilt; the need to *please*; the fear of *rejection*: despite my happy upbringing, I still experienced these three desperate emotions.

My mother worried about me, protected me and wanted only the best to happen to me. But the impact of her mothering was magnified by my being the last in line and amplified all the more because I was still very young when my siblings had flown the nest.

My mum grew up in a large family of five with a mother whose own upbringing had made of her an admirable stoic. My mother suffered from this more than she can say and compensated for her lacking warmth at home by turning ours into a sanctuary. Once again, that feeling of living in the cosiest, safest place on earth resonated with all the more powerful an echo once it was just me occupying that space. My mother, my father, and me.

I remember vividly when the time came for me to spend a full day at nursery school: I burst into tears and ran to the door, clinging to my mummy's knees. I loved my school, but a whole day felt much too long away from home, away from her. By her side was where I liked to be best of all. It still is so often. So she found a way to make me feel safe. A compromise that would make the worries disappear. My mother came to fetch me at our scheduled snoozing-time and dropped me off again when the rest of my class was due to wake. Daily. That way I could snuggle in my own bed.

When I was six or seven my school organised our very first field trip in the mountains, an hour and a half away from home. It was an overnight excursion, or perhaps we were even to spend more than one night away; I don't remember for sure. The great big buses were parked neatly outside the gates and their purring engines bid us to jump on board. I followed my classmates and scrambled inside, waving just like everyone else to all our little mothers beaming brave smiles in the hope that we might catch a flicker or two. The doors slid shut and the wheels turned to roll forward. Then this little girl bounced out of her seat, made the bus stop and leaped right back out to her mummy safe and sound. My mother therefore drove me all the way to our campsite, made sure I was safely installed, then left me alone. From then on, and until we had reached the year when such school trips no longer took place, my mum drove me to every chosen destination, separate from everyone else, in the comfort of our own car, settled me down and eventually drove off. Like this, she made it all okay.

I could always have all the friends I wanted over to play, for sleepovers, to watch movies with pizzas and to have a midnight feast. The house was always open to anyone who wanted to drop by. But when it came to my asking permission to stay at my friends' homes, that was more difficult. There were few other households that my mother trusted to be suitable and safe enough to let me go, even if only for one night. She liked to drop me off because that way she could rest assured that I was going to be okay. I know, again, that she did this only with the best of intentions at heart. But maybe it was time for her to let go and for the message to be more that I would be okay no matter what, rather than the anticipated nightmare of my being unhappy, or emotionally bruised. Because bruises generally fade away and once in a while we need to know what it feels like to stumble and get ourselves back on our own two feet.

The truth is, actually, that with all the love I received, from my family from the moment I was born, and with all the love I continued to receive on a daily basis from so many more in time, there was an extra-super-padded safety net already in place to catch me should I ever fall. In fact, without it I would not be writing this book today.

The picture I am drawing is one of a mother who wanted so much for her delicate, sensitive little girl to be loved, and sheltered from the risk of potential harm. And all the caring a mother ever could give was poured down on me twice as much once my siblings had left the house. And her attention was even more pronounced because though I was an altogether joyful, cheery child, my exuberance was wrapped in a very thin skin. And this she knew.

There is a visceral bond that ties me to my mother. Perhaps the reason for this is because she almost lost me when she was pregnant. Whenever she feels sad I tend to feel the same. Whenever I feel upset it turns out she too is having a bad day. When I have a headache more often than not I will call and her skull is pounding too. We feed off each other's bad days and build on each other's good. My mother is receptive to any sadness in the atmosphere. That is an attribute that came to me straight through the umbilical cord. Between the two of us there is a reception signal running more clearly than with anyone else, and it is on constant alert.

Some might call this co-dependency and suggest that clearer boundaries need to be drawn. This might be true. But how do you begin to dissect an affection so deep? And where do you strike the balance between a 'healthy' relationship and one that has become 'blurred'? Who has the presumption to establish rules in love?

I love my maman, more than words can say. She taught me to be forgiving and never to fall asleep on a frown. My mother has always been my stronghold, my shield. She is faithful, dependable, reliable, funny, clumsy sometimes, scrupulous yet hasty, enduring yet impatient: touching. And I see so much of me in her. She never lost faith in me, not once. That faith was a torch that brought me back on track. The trust she has always had in my capacity to flourish, come what may, was a beacon of hope that kept me standing, that keeps me going.

I remember once, when I was eight years old, waking up to the sound of maman crying in her bathroom. Her bathroom wall adjoined that of my bedroom and from my pillow I heard her weep. My grandfather had died. That was my first encounter with death, yet the only vivid memory I have of the time is that of waking up to the sound of my mother's tears.

It was when I was aged fifteen, that my mummy lost her laugh. The memory is patchy and there are only snippets I can grasp to pull together a picture of what it felt like at the time. But the image that jumps out at me over and over again is finding her in bed or on the sofa, lying there in desolation, day after day. And she would never last for more than ten minutes at dinner with us, fiddling with her food, often shedding tears before leaving the table. I remember her craving pancakes and sautéed potatoes. But neither the sweetness nor the starch seemed enough to cushion the pain. She was helpless, unable to master the inexplicable ache that was searing her inside – and it was beginning to filter through to her little girl.

I would be at school, in French class, perhaps, sitting by the window, making a mental list of all the things I wanted to do with maman to make her smile. I'd take her to the cinema; I would go for a long walk with her and sit by her side, or we could bake a cake together and have a dough fight, too.

I would come home from school every day with a plan to make it all okay … And then I would open the door, and she would be there, and I would turn cold and my good intentions would vanish and I would trample over my patience as I said hello. Perhaps if I gave her reason to take care of me she might crack her shell? Perhaps if I gave her reason enough to worry about me she would have no time to worry about herself any more?

I liked to make things right. I was the one who went cycling around the neighbourhood in search of animals to rescue. I was the one whose Christmas list ended with wishes of peace on earth and health for everyone. I hated the thought of people suffering, fighting, hating, hurting – I wanted to help make it all okay; but this time I couldn't. And if I couldn't make it okay then did that mean I was the cause for it *not* being okay?

And so feelings of guilt and shame began to envelop me,

and then came feelings of self-reproach. All primary feelings in any anorexic tale. All key to the story I want to tell. A sense of uncertainty that first came, perhaps, with the shaking of my mother, the rock: my rock.

28 November 1999 (aged 16)

It's amazing how one constructs the image, the ideal, the icon of what one wants certain key figures to be. It's crazy how hard it is when that image falls to pieces, when the lights turn on and the screen goes blank. This weekend I realised that my mother is so very fragile and that she too can be sick and tired and hurt. And the truth of the matter is that we're all human beings at the end of the day, and that nobody is perfect, not even my family, not even me, not even what I want them and I to be.

I didn't become anorexic overnight, and it didn't happen there and then. It took a while before it all became symptomatic. But symptoms are just that: they tell you that something has happened, they do not tell you why.

My mother's anxieties were *not* the only factor that led

me, in turn, to go through my dismal days. In fact, the more I look into this, the more I realise how impossible it is to boil it down to an obvious sequential system of logical events. I am not blaming anyone for anything. The point of this book is neither to play a blame game nor a shame game, nor any game of guilt.

But seeing my mother lose her laugh made me feel sad, lonely, afraid, guilty, hurt and perhaps even angry at times (it will take me far beyond the pages of this book fully to come to terms with those emotions). And for the very first time, I no longer felt safe.

And then there is my sister, Amanda.

It is difficult not to mention my sister when I analyse my behaviour towards myself, but it is just as hard to find the right words to describe our relationship, the ones that tell without guilt.

I am naturally inclined to feel self-conscious and concerned, always, about how others might perceive me, that what I say might be misunderstood. And I'm particularly concerned and self-conscious around my sister. For years I walked on eggshells around her for fear of making a mistake, causing conflict somehow or getting on her wrong side.

My sister is older than me, by eleven years. She is petite, perfectly proportioned, dresses immaculately, never appears to have a blemish, always looks fresh, she has perfect posture and two beautiful children who are equally perfect. I sit next to her and I cannot help but feel just a little shabby, a touch clumsy, altogether 'not-quite-right'. She does nothing, nothing at all, to make me feel this way – and yet, I do.

When I was a little girl, she was my role model and I was her baby doll. It was tender and fond, without question. But as I grew up, there crept in an awkward change in our relationship. As the baby doll took to looking in the mirror, so her gaze reached beyond her reflection to that of her big sister. And then one day I was no longer simply looking up to her in wonder and awe, but comparing my smaller self with the perfect image of her that I had created.

There is one picture taken of us by the pool. I must be about fifteen. We are interlaced in hugs, both wearing swimming suits. I always hated that photograph and I still do today. She is sitting upright in a bikini, her head held high, her hair is wet and perfectly tied back, her stomach is toned. She is golden-brown, not burnt; her smile reveals shining white teeth, perfectly aligned. She looks perfect. I am wearing a one-piece suit, orange, which clashes with my skin tone. I am slouching to her level, I look awkward, disjointed almost, my smile is ungainly. I look big and ugly and I hate myself.

Perfect

I was recently reminded by a friend how often I used to speak about my sister with words of adulation – and traces of self-contempt. How well she had performed in school, then Oxford, then her masters, then Sotheby's; all in a straight line. She wanted children by the age of twenty-eight; she had her first baby halfway through her twenty-eighth year. A perfect trajectory I somehow feared to follow – or fail in following.

I write about my sister and inevitably that sense of guilt takes over. I want to be able to paint an outline of our relationship without filling in the details – I don't want anyone to misunderstand or misread our relationship and there are certain things that must remain private. What I want to say, because I believe this applies to so many other sisters, is that it was – and is – my *own* perception that needs looking into. *I* need to learn to feel comfortable enough with the face I see reflected back at me not to compare that vision to her.

I thought for a long time that my relationship with my sister (or the impression of her that I created over time) might have been an instigating factor that set me down the path of anorexia. Because of that I often distanced myself from her, unjustly, when I was unwell. But I realise today that the way I feel when my sister is sitting by my side differs dramatically from one day to the next, according to how I am feeling about myself, and that, instead of being a cause, any negativity is an indicator that there is a cloud hanging over my own heart.

Simply put, it's all about me learning to feel comfortable with myself. Amanda is my sister, but above all she is herself. I now need also to find the same security – around her, around anyone, around myself. And that is the point.

❧

Looking back, I remember how happy I was as a child. I had forgotten. I was full of joy, full of life. I was cheeky, eccentric, creative and with a mind that floated on a cloud. I loved to act silly, laugh till my stomach hurt, put on shows, write plays, invent stories, run around outside, roller-skate, ride my bike with a little radio fixed to the seat, make up recipes, bake cakes, then cuddle up in front of a family movie on a Sunday night, with take-out hamburgers, ketchup and chips. Family holidays were filled with smiles. Family and friends: my life summed up in two words.

I was sensitive, passionate. I grew up and I fell in love, cried heartbroken over gorgeous boys, listened to dreamy music, wrote letters that smacked of all things sweet. I was a hopeless romantic and an idealist at heart: I wanted to make the world a better place. As a teenager I wore all sorts of crazy outfits and went out dancing till the break of dawn. I had the odd drink too many, skipped class once in a while. I did not lie to my parents though. I do not lie. But still I was mischievous and impertinent at times – though not disrespectful, ever. I was happy.

These past few years I have become so engrossed with this disease, so focused on trying to understand why and when I suddenly became so serious, that I somehow stripped my memory bare of the way things were before the shift occurred. I was a lively, happy little girl

Anorexia is not merely about body dysmorphia. There is a far deeper-reaching perversion of the mind that occurs when you are caught within the grips of this beast. You forget yourself.

I never want to forget myself again.

2

I don't think I could write a book about my struggle with anorexia without touching on the time it became manifestly clear. I wish there were a way for me only to tell the story of what goes on beneath the surface; inside of the emaciated shell. I am so reluctant to fuel such sensational headlines as 'Dying to be Thin' or 'Media Strikes Again: Pressures of a society ruled by shape and size'. I worry that people may latch on to what I am about to tell, seeing it as the reason for my long battle with anorexia, when the underlying causes are much more complicated than what the following lines describe. And yet, this book would be incomplete if I didn't tell this part too.

My memories of childhood and food are not ones of restriction, nor were any treats banned; I knew where to draw the line between naughty treats and healthy eats. My mother practised yoga and studied a holistic approach to food for several years before I was born. There are so many flavours that spring to mind when I think of me as a little girl: caramel ice cream; lemon-sugar crêpes; Nutella; green M&Ms; candy canes at Christmas; pasta with ketchup-soya sauce-parmesan cheese and peas (I have always loved peas); chocolate muesli with an extra cheeky spoonful of dark brown muscovado sugar; warm Ovaltine in a baby bottle; porridge with maple syrup; yellow pizzas (omelette); risotto; artichokes and vinaigrette; chips and burgers on a Sunday – yum! The mere thought of these sends warmth to my stomach and makes me want to cuddle up all cosy in front of a feel-good movie on TV. They were among the first to be struck through with a clear black line, and they are still the last to reappear easily on my current list of foods. These things take time.

Physical signs of what might already have been an underlying disease started to surface about a year after my mother's anxiety attacks had hit her – us – hard. I cannot say when the slope gradually headed downwards nor at what point its incline became steep enough for me to slip. I know I was just a regular sixteen-year-old, going out, having fun, falling in love, and heartbroken over and over. I know I started to think about my weight because all the other girls would talk about their size and it is true that both magazines and sitcoms paraded idols, all pretty, slender and cool. Still, I never really stopped to think about the size of my jeans and was lucky enough that most outfits suited me. I enjoyed eating and was renowned for midnight snacks at sleepovers with friends: a pizza topped with parmesan cheese or a plateful of pasta covered in ketchup. And I can't say exactly when all that started to stop.

I began to ask permission to have a bowl of muesli at night rather than share a meal with everyone else. It was granted because it all fell under the expectation of what a regular sixteen-year-old goes through: going on a diet was a fleeting fad alongside boys, make-up, parties and occasional uprisings: nothing serious. But when *did* it become serious? And when did *I* suddenly become so serious? I wish I knew. Then there was the fashion show.

The fashion show is, unfortunately, what most would mention as when I toppled over the fence into anorexia, even as I may, in fact, have been dancing on its narrow beams for far longer before. That was when it really became apparent, from the outside – on the outside – that all, that I, was not well.

It was a silly school affair: there was no real selection procedure nor any real fear of elimination. All the clothes were designed by the students as part of their art class final assessment. I had participated the year before and that was fun, just fun. But in my penultimate year of high school, I was now chosen to wear the wedding dress. This was the dress of dreams and would involve grace, elegance and refinement. The dress was made to measure, so I had to make sure I kept that figure upon which it had been stitched. The wedding dress was beautiful, and I had to do everything I could to match its beauty. Alongside the wedding dress I had also been asked to model an Indian outfit: a long floating green silk skirt with a scarf tied to cover my breasts and little else. The skirt had been made by an Indian friend – she had bought the fabric and made the final touches in India– it was ornate with tremendous detail: there was no way of altering the skirt that had been specially hand-sewn. But the model that had been used for measurements cannot have had much to eat that day – and whoever was destined to wear it could not afford to gain any weight either. So many girls tried it on, but not one could fasten its clip around her waist. Then I tried it on, and in a Cinderella moment it fit. My tummy was sucked in but I could still breathe.

It began as just a temporary shift in my usual dietary habits so that I wouldn't crack the stitchings on the skirt. I couldn't feel myself slip into the disease; I didn't see that I was slipping at all. From the time rehearsals began till my last stride down the catwalk, that would be as far as my new eating regimen would go. Then the spotlight would switch off and my normal life would resume, unaffected.

But in reality I had caught the disease by then. And though neither I, nor my parents, noticed anything yet, my fever was actually constantly on the rise.

My bowl of muesli for dinner remained, but it was no longer supplemented with wholesome creamy yoghurt and an extra sprinkle of sugar for good measure. There began an imperceptible filtering of ingredients, one by one, sifted through and sorted out. I don't even remember which were first to appear on the index of forbidden foods, it was all hardly noticeable and highly unremarkable at the time. I had a set date in mind as to when I could once more allow myself to pick and choose from the list of meals crossed out. As soon as the fashion show ended that was it. This was my secret promise. The truth is, it all happened so fast and yet at such a snail's pace at the same time. I was hoodwinked along with everyone else.

As weeks flew by, so more food options took flight. I see it now, like a spiral staircase I was spinning down, blindly. This was how my meals were gradually being whittled down:

Step 1: Special K for breakfast with semi-skimmed milk and a dash of sugar; salad with a piece of bread and butter for lunch; a bowl of muesli with yoghurt for dinner and a fruit salad

Step 2: Special K for breakfast with semi-skimmed milk and no sugar; salad for lunch with one slice of bread and no butter; a bowl of muesli with yoghurt for dinner – no fruit salad tonight

Step 3: All-Bran with skimmed milk for breakfast; salad with no dressing for lunch; muesli with fat-free yoghurt for dinner

Step 4: All-Bran and skimmed milk cut with water for breakfast; an apple for lunch; a lighter choice of cereal for dinner

Step 5: All-Bran and water for breakfast, lots and lots of All-Bran to 'get the digestive system going'; apple for lunch; cereal for dinner

Weekends were a bit more difficult because I was at home and I could not hide my food choices so easily. So I drew up a set of physical exercises to balance out any dietary lapse: sit-ups, swimming and walking could all be fitted into a daily routine with reasonable ease. These, however, were becoming part of a greater calculation, the pluses of exercise and the minuses of food, one I thought I was managing myself, but which was already being dictated by a Greater Voice.

Meanwhile, I took the worthy and respectable decision of adhering strictly to Lent that year – I would have no chocolate for fifty days and it was solely for decent reasons of faith. I was at one of our fashion show rehearsals which, being a school fashion show run by students for students, was a rehearsal filled with sweets, chocolate bars, crisps and fizzy drinks. After an afternoon's worth of 'no thank you's and 'I'll be fine thank you very much's, I finally decided I ought to have *one* M&M. It was the peanut kind, green for good luck. We have a tradition in our family always to have a green M&M before travelling, a superstition I relished as a child and the sort of familiar practice that makes you feel a part of something secretly special. So here was to good fortune. I briefly delighted in my delicacy; I sucked at the blessed sugary green coating then eventually bit through the now softened shell, into the melting chocolate and crunched at the peanut inside. It was delicious and I was soon overcome with guilt at my sin. I felt ashamed at having given in and began furiously to discuss the implications of my indulgence with a friend, anxious for reassurance and hopeful that my immediate confession might be enough to redeem the errant act. Our conversation focused entirely on the repercussions of my slip in Lent. My friend was as oblivious as I to the fact that something – *someone* – else had long taken God's place. From then on I stuck to my resolution with determination and felt an indescribable inner strength grow each day I did not succumb to any temptation.

'Cruella' was how I soon would come to name that 'someone'. For now she was still an unknown voice; her whispers in my ear were still subtle enough that I mistook them for my own. Later, once it became – or was made – clearer to me that I was ill and needed help, I gave my illness a name; this allowed me – and my family – to distance ourselves from it. It felt so much like being possessed by a diabolical force. There was a voice that whispered twisted suggestions in my ear and persuaded me to act or think in ways I could not recognise as my own. She was pure evil. She was Cruella; a silly childhood villain that had always haunted me from a book that remains one of my favourites to this day. But giving the voice a name helped me so much to visualise my battle, and once she was named it helped everyone around me to see the voice as less violent, perhaps, less frightening, more easily pictured for those who found it all too difficult to grasp.

But Cruella was in the future. In the weeks leading up to the fashion show any extravagance came at a cost. Anything outside my daily allowance had its price. There was less and less room in my world for conversations with friends, unwinding over a cup of tea, settling down in front of a film or with a good book to read. All this space was occupied by incessant calculations, filled with evaluation, estimation, compensation against any eventual momentary lapse. Perhaps that was the highest cost of all.

1 apple on top of breakfast = *1 hour walk all the way down town and all the way back up*

1 extra handful of All Bran = *50 laps in the pool, without a pause*

1 more dried apricot = *100 sit ups on top of the daily routine (minimum 200)*

1 tbsp couscous = *30 min brisk march round and
round the block until I feel light again*
3 more strawberries at lunch = *0 dessert for dinner*

Restrain, check, restrict, constrain, control, check =
Discipline

Trickle by trickle the pounds began to shed. Family began to notice. Friends began to talk. Whispers could be overheard and the feeling was one of immense satisfaction. Any friendly mention of concern was welcomed with a smile of reassurance and quietly ignored. Progressively, item after item of my wardrobe slowly slipped down my hips and dragged along the floor as I obsessively walked myself slim.

At lunch, I could be found walking back home for a swim or in the library for mental gymnastics. My attitude to studies went hand in hand with the painstaking set of rules I had imposed on the rest of myself. In the past I had never been a conscientious, hard-working student. I always did what it took to do well and generally got along with those teachers who taught those subjects I enjoyed. I did not sit at the front of the classroom and the notes I scribbled were more often than not intended for a friend sitting a few desks down. But all that changed with my new eating regimen. Soon my every assignment would not be faulted. Now I was competing against myself, needing to outdo myself, striving to be perfect. And as the desire to be with friends lessened with time, so my books became my unparalleled companions.

It was a few days before the Fashion Show started: the dress rehearsal. We hadn't worn our clothes since they had first been measured. It was the final fitting – and the idea was not to alter the fit. The wedding dress looked beautiful, and it slipped right on. And then it slipped right off. I took a deep breath in and pumped up my chest so it was filled with air and ballooned like the top end of a corset. But the dress slipped off again. More whispers, arrowed glances darting through the room – a couple hitting me and making it hard to hold back the tears. I flushed what little blood I could summon to my hollowed cheeks. The dress was duly taken in.

Lights off. Let the show begin. My parents were sitting in front row, and next to them sat my brother. The show was over almost before I knew it; all eyes staring; spotlight blocking out the opinions I cared for most – my mother's, my father's and my brother's. I returned home and everyone was sat at the kitchen table, having had dinner already and chatting happily away. As I entered I felt an unspoken chill send shivers down my spine.

It came less from my parents, more from my brother. Patrick had been so complimentary of me the year before and had enjoyed the show so much. I valued – I value – his esteem for me and his appreciation of the person that I am enormously. He is my Big Brother and has earned the capitalisation of his title by being the first to take me out for a night of fun, the one with whom I shared my first naughty drink and the shoulder upon which I rested my first tipsy cheek! He was the one I turned to for advice and I felt so thrilled that I, in turn, was always privy to secrets of his that nobody else could know. Patrick made me feel beautiful, special, loved. All feelings that were beginning to feel foreign to me.

But that night, Patrick did not smile when I came home, and there was no flattering remark offered from him. That, perhaps, was the first moment I stopped to question the integrity of my performance, both onstage and off.

My parents were encouraging though not overly enthusiastic: I did not shine. I was not acclaimed. An awkward hush filled the house – and it told more than words could yet dare to say. Come the last night of the show, my mind was fixed on the one promise I was determined to keep. A promise I made myself – and one which I was looking forward to desperately. The one that certified a swift and happy return to unrestricted eating patterns as soon as the spotlights were cut.

Final catwalk, last round of applause, dressing rooms filled with chatter, celebration and excitement at the thought of a fun night ahead. But the voices were muffled and the thrill a mere agitation set against my long-awaited ecstasy: I took a bite out of my slice of pizza. And I began to shake inside. A second bite, trying not to chew, trying to enjoy the sensation without fearing the idea. Gulp, gulp, gulp. But my head was already spinning and now the only voices I could hear were pinching me with guilt. And so I danced the night away. I danced and danced till the pizza slice floated away. And then I danced some more, so the sense of emptiness came back; that comforting feeling of hollow inside.

I later found out that my friend, the one who designed the wedding dress and who took the dress in, went to speak to my parents at the opening night and voiced her concerns. They listened. They thanked her. They may even have heard what she said. But what lay beneath her words was just too big to be applicable to their good, sweet, happy, smiling, lively little girl.

The Fashion Show was how it came to the surface. This was not how it began. This was not where it began. This was where it became apparent and this, perhaps, was where it earned its name. It is the most tangible way to tell the story because it is the sensational way: when people can picture the scene and measure the gravity of the situation by the image they have in mind. But these were – are – mere symptoms. It was not about being thin; it was not about fitting the dress; it was not about walking the walk and it was not about magazines, television or diet pill ads.

I want to take the opportunity to underline, once more, that the fashion show merely acted as a hook upon which drapes of underlying issues were fixed. The fashion show offered an accidental opportunity for whatever was going on inside finally to manifest itself to the outside world. The fashion show was *not* the cause for my anorexia. I wish, in a sense, that it could all be so simple. Surely then it would be just as easy to determine a definitive, universal, solution to the problem once and for all. But it isn't that clear cut — and that is all too easy to forget.

By the end of the fashion show it became a little clearer to me that I wasn't calling the shots. My game-plan, or so I had believed, was to end this little challenge of mine come closing of the curtain. That night I felt a fear, because suddenly I was no longer able to play by my own rules; suddenly I began to feel that I was being played with. But I had no notion of what an eating disorder involved; it had never officially been discussed at school, only spoken about with grand sweeping exclamations of horror and disgust. I had never been moved to think beyond an initial gut reaction of shock whenever I saw such dreadful skeletons walking down the street. And those were images, ghastly images, that did not pertain to me. So there really was nothing to worry about at all.

3

A few months later and school was out for summer. Still, nothing had changed. I became more and more advanced in the skill of mental arithmetic. Simply put, it was a matter of subtracting physical expenditure from calorific intake and to achieve an end result that went below zero (daily calories spent 1000 – daily physical exertion worth 2500 calories = -1500 = weightloss). But still, it all just felt like some kind of a game. One from which I would walk away once I grew bored of rolling dice. Nothing dangerous. No risks taken. Just a silly, trivial, game.

We went on holiday together, as a family, to our home in Italy, where we went every year. Nothing scary, nothing unknown, nothing unexpected. As before, I made myself the promise that when I was away I would savour the smell, delight in the taste and relish the pleasure of the food I loved most of all. And all this restrictive behaviour would duly come to an end. I had a list of ultimate desires that I brought with me, neatly folded in my diary, painstakingly inscribed with a brightly coloured felt-tip pen: *ice cream, pasta, pesto, foccaccia, pizza*. One luxury a day; treats long awaited and suitably deserved.

I told myself that if my friends in Italy seemed shocked, having not seen me for a year, if they also said I had lost too much weight, then I would let the alarm bells ring loud and clear; then I would consider reassessing my new way of eating. That was the benchmark I now had drawn to reach a verdict as to whether or not this had all gone too far, though exactly what 'this' was I still could not say. I was putting off decisions to tomorrow, and tomorrow never came.

These friends, one after the other, told me I had slimmed down, each with that same troubled look. I reassured them with a sweet smile that I had had a difficult year and that I was going to be okay. It was a stupid decision anyway to base my lifestyle on the way others perceived me. Tomorrow I might heed their concerns; today I had no time. Meanwhile, night came and went and my list of target foods remained immaculate; not a tick, not a word crossed out, not a sign to proclaim that any milestones were reached or progress made. Sitting at table for dinner became my most dreaded moment of the day; and my day was spent calculating how to avoid any glance at my plate.

I was lying on the beach, soaking in the sun for a body that was beginning to feel cold so often. Eyes shut, looking to relax, just a little. My father came to sit by my side. He spoke. I listened, and for once I heard the fear in his voice. This time it sent shivers down my spine. My father belongs to the medical faculty; he is a professor in medicine. He was serious. And his seriousness made me afraid of myself. I am enormously close to my father and value his opinion, both in general and of me, with the greatest amount of respect. Although he appears stern to those who meet him for the very first time, I see beyond the mask. My father is loving, sensitive, compassionate and he has such a deep under-standing of me. I care so much (too much?) about making him proud and have always hated the idea of disappointing him though he has never made me feel like I ever could.

'Babs, your mother and I are now really concerned. I am worried that your weight loss could be causing irreparable damage to your body. I suspect you are now at a stage where you are suffering from several deficiencies and that your body is hungry for nutrients. Above all, I hate to see you looking like this.'

These weren't his exact words, as I don't remember them verbatim, and I do not recall my precise reaction. I only remember the tingling feeling of fear that prickled in my spine and tickled all the way through to my fingertips. So far my friends had told me I should put on weight and suggested something wasn't right. Till then my parents had not voiced any real distress. There was an elephant in every room, growing bigger by the day, of which no one so far had dared to speak. I could feel it because our family is close enough that these things are quickly detected. But as long as nothing was said I chose, conveniently, to believe that the elephant was a mere figment of my imagination, and that no one else knew that it was there.

When my father came to speak to me I did not try to argue. But I felt I had reached a stage where only a doctor could spell things out. I now required medical proof that something was terribly wrong and a medical prescription to solve it. If it turned out that I was indeed depleted of essential vitamins and minerals, then it was game over. But I still could not tell what game it was I was playing, nor that I had become a pawn.

I agreed to see a doctor upon our return home. I agreed to blood tests to make sure that I was not severely deficient in elements essential to my health. Blood tests: these were serious. I think I knew I needed this examination; some sort of medical wake-up call that could shake me out of this stand-still I seemed to have reached. To pull me out of the spiral down which I was beginning to feel myself dwindle and drop.

My parents made an appointment and once we were back from Italy I went to the doctor. Feeling dizzy before the needle went in, I pulled up my sleeve and looked away. My heart pumped what it could; it slowed to a couple of heavy thuds and enough red liquid was drawn so that they might examine its content and tell me I had taken it all too far. But they didn't. A few days later I was sat at the doctor's mahogany desk and learned that my measures of vitamins and minerals were all within normal range. It was suggested to me that perhaps I consider adding a spoonful more cornflakes to my bowl in the morning and that I pour whole-fat milk on top, rather than diluted skimmed. The irony of it all was that I hadn't set out to fool anyone; a side of me almost hoped that if my ears were pulled hard enough by someone qualified who held hard evidence that my body was shutting down, then maybe I could side with the authority and hush *her* voice. But the judge, it seemed, had sided with the felon.

It was a conversation with my brother that eventually led me to take the steps necessary to find a way for it all to start to stop. He was on the phone from New York and he knew that I was slipping. Vanessa, his girlfriend at the time, had walked the same line a few years back and he suggested that I talk to her as someone who could relate to me and with whom I could identify. Vanessa had seen a psychiatrist at the hospital in Geneva and this woman's reputation was impressive. So I wrote to Vanessa. If she, who apparently had been through something similar, recognised that I was not just being a teenage girl but that something bigger was happening to me, if she voiced concern all the way from New York without ever having met me, *then* I would agree to see someone serious who could tell me why my heart felt so tight, why my throat would always choke, why I found it hard to reach for a smile and why I found such comfort in that dark, empty, hungry space inside.

To Vanessa 15 August 2000 (aged 17)

I don't know where to begin really, if I did I suppose I would have less difficulty getting out of this 'mess' in the first place. When I look at myself in a mirror I do not see a plump little girl who still has a long way to go before resembling someone on America's Next Top Model. *I do realise that I am too thin, at least I think I do. When it comes to taking action though, things are not as simple as the resolutions I had taken tended to suggest. For so long now (exactly how long and why I cannot tell), I have excluded from my diet virtually all 'fat' products i.e., whole milk, whole milk yoghurts, cheese, butter … Taking the step to actually swallow any of the above remains a very difficult task even if I know that I should. It's like in cartoons when you have a little angel in a cloud on one side and a little devil in a flame on the other. One force is telling me that I have to get out of this as soon as possible and that unless I pull myself together and get back into healthy habits I will keep on drifting further away from the target. Yet the other force is restraining me. Although my little devil has absolutely no argument to stand on and my little angel should in theory be much more persuasive, somehow the little rascal always seems to win. When it comes to eating fruit and vegetables there is absolutely no problem: wholegrain bread and cereals all go down fine. But I have developed this obsession of scanning the ingredients and percentage of fat contained in whatever we buy. Supermarkets take twice the time and effort as they used to and I can deal less and less with going out to the restaurant or for a meal at someone's house for fear of not knowing exactly what has gone into their food. Some days though, are better than others. The thing is, and this is both an advantage and a disadvantage, I have quite a lot of knowledge biologically/dietetically wise. The point being that I know what is good and not good for me and my health, but I also know what a lipid is, what a carbohydrate is, where they are found and what they do. Sometimes I wish I were a little less clued-up on that level so that when offered a slice of ham I might eat it without having to dissect any trace of a white streak that would signal some fat. I wish I weren't so apprehensive to the point of tears at the mere thought of being presented with a meal containing a combination of meat and carbs. It's weird because it's not that I don't want to eat, it's like I am hungry but have no appetite, and I have trouble in determining whether what I am eating is enough, too much or too little.*

I feel much more fragile physically, but above all emotionally – and that is saying a lot given that in my 'normal' frame of mind you could have me in floods of tears just watching Mrs Doubtfire! *Now I cry whenever, wherever and for whatever reason. I feel vulnerable and often have panic attacks. Conclusion, this year has seen me recoil into my little family nest; I have been going out less and less, secluding myself from many of my friends – and probably losing them too. It's not that I'm a goodie two-shoes who wants to stay at home and read her books (although I do love books!), it's just that I get tired more quickly and that I don't feel 'at home' with almost anybody. But I guess now the summer holiday is nearly over and no one has seen anyone in two months means that I will be able to start a fresh new school year. I suppose I'm just going through a stage in my life in which a lot is occurring, notably the International Baccalaureate, university applications, (university itself!) … and it's getting to me a little more strongly than it perhaps should; maybe it's all a little less dramatic than it is beginning to seem …* I just don't know!

Vanessa's reply 17 August 2000

Dear Emily,

Your email really touched me in many ways. I found myself in your words. When I first started eating less and being self-conscious about my weight I did not really think much of it. That was about four years ago. However, I, along with many of my close friends and family, noticed that anything that had oil, butter, cream, cheese, any type of sauce etc., disgusted me and had been banned from my diet. Anything water-based, healthy and virtually empty of much calorific value was what I had accustomed my stomach to receive. Needless to say that as a result this little stomach of mine had lost the ability to think for itself. It became a vicious cycle, the less I ate the less room there was for an appetite, and meanwhile my hunger was growing too.

Furthermore, I had lost all sense of enjoyment when it came to food, and I lost all sense of proportion – a tiny bit of this and a tiny bit of that seemed and was more than enough to have me saying, 'No thank you, that's enough, anyways I'm not even all that hungry.' The problem with all of this was that I soon found out that my body was beginning to lack in quite a few important nutrients. That also explained my fatigue and most of all how sensitive and touchy I had become...

There is one last tip I want to leave you with to mull. If you can, try to eat one thing a day that you used to enjoy and recently cut out. It needn't be in gargantuan quantities. Start with just a bite – so you can see that it doesn't bite back! This way, slowly and surely, your body will get used to

*a little variety once more, and progressively trust, in
yourself, in your food, will build again.*

To Vanessa 24 August 2000

*… I feel like things are getting better right now, I am really
trying to give myself a kick, not so much for myself but
rather for my surroundings – notably my parents who do not
deserve to go through this. All the same, there are days with
and there are days without. Your suggestion of trying or
reintroducing a new food each day is a good idea but to be
honest with you it is not so easy in practice. Every time I ask
myself what I could add I then skim down the list, crossing
out one possibility after the other, from ice cream to butter to
chocolate. I had a moment of panic when I got back from
Olivia's in the South of France (where I didn't eat much
because I wasn't at home and the food was all very heavy)
and I weighed myself to find that I had dropped to 39.5kg;
the point is that the doctor told me that if I went below
40kg we were going to have to take all this a little more
seriously. The following morning I weighed myself again and
was back to 40.5kg (still 2–3kg less than before I left). I
need you to know that I have told nobody what I am telling
you, but that I need to spill it all out on someone and you*

are my only resort right now. In fact, I wanted to ask you a question to which you are absolutely not obliged to answer but that might help me to situate myself on the grand scheme of danger-zones: how much did you weigh when it became 'serious' and you went to see somebody? I would also like to know whether these are 'symptomatic' behaviours: I cannot bear to eat alone anymore, I need to eat with someone else so that I can measure the amount of food I serve on my plate to that of the person I am eating with (i.e. that they are always eating more than me). I have developed an obsession of constantly looking forward to the next meal of the day; I fall asleep thinking about what I will have for breakfast and where I might go have lunch with my mum (and on that note, I wake up so much earlier than I used to because I cannot sleep but also so as to ensure that my digestion functions as well as possible); I have to be with my mum when she is shopping for food and planning dinner so that I can check and control exactly what is going on; on mornings when I crave an extra piece of fruit, I will allow myself only with a promise of having that much less at lunch; then at lunch I will allow myself any extra mouthful on the condition that I walk however many miles it will take to make me feel 'purged'; if I feel like a second serving of anything but my plate is taken away before I move to help myself I take it as a sign that I wasn't to have that and I was being excessive; if we are having a meal with which I do not

*agree and I know my plate will be checked to make sure I
am having more than just vegetables, I will have a bit of the
'mean' food and cover it with heaps of 'good' stuff to make it
seem as though there is more underneath and for my plate to
seem appropriately full, or I will talk and talk to avoid
glances at my plate and comments about what I am eating.
I can always be found in the kitchen when meals are being
prepared so I can control exactly how each food is being
cooked and somehow push for steaming over anything
involving oil. Finally, I have come to dread weekends when
my father cooks because he tends to add more fatty
substances in the food than Myriam (our cleaning lady)
does, now more than ever because he is 'on my case' (and I
am not saying this in a blaming, malicious way). Once my
daddy's food used to be my favourite in the world. One last
thing come to think of it, my new thing is to pretend to have
developed dislikes for things I once loved. Just the other day
my sister asked me if I wanted some feta cheese (which I
used to enjoy) in a Greek salad and I told her that for some
reason I wasn't such a fan of feta anymore. The other day we
were at the restaurant with my parents and grandmother
and when it was time to order dessert I said it all looked a
little too fancy for me. When I saw that hadn't really worked
and that my mum was pushing me with suggestions of
things she knew belonged to my list of favourites, I then
announced 'Thank God I didn't stay any longer in the sun*

today because I am feeling a little queasy.' My mum, I
think, didn't really believe a word of it but my dad actually
went so far as to apologise, 'And there I was thinking that
you were calorie-counting.' I have never in my life felt so
bad as I did at that moment when I saw that he genuinely
believed me and I was deceiving him, I swore to myself that
I would tell him the truth one day. Vanessa, I am so sorry
for spilling all my secrets out to you. I never thought I would
ever tell anybody all this, except perhaps my daughter one
day if she should go through the same (provided I have a
daughter considering how long it's been since my last
period). It feels good to get this all out on paper, and a good
thing too that I am shocked at the description of my very
own behaviour as I write. I should add that I have
condensed everything into one and that there are days when
I am able to control all this and avoid the worst.

Vanessa's reply 27 August 2000

Dear Emily,
There are no two ways about how to say this, I am going to
be honest and straight forward: I am worried. I am not a
professional and therefore do not necessarily know what to
say and what not to say, how best to say it and how not to say

it. But what I know comes straight from my heart and from what I have learned through my own experience … I feel privileged that you have confided in me with such ease and trust, but I am so far away and feel so helpless. I would love for you to also (don't get me wrong, I by no means mean for you to stop telling me anything and everything you want) see somebody that is more qualified. I care so much about you and it hurts me to see you like this. Moreover, by telling me certain things that you might not have told other people, I feel a great sense of responsibility and cannot simply listen. I must tell you my honest opinion.

You mentioned in the email that you were trying to push yourself 'not so much for you but rather for your surroundings – notably your parents who do not deserve to go through this'. Let me tell you that your primary concern is yourself, you cannot start thinking about everyone else, and above all you have to do this for yourself. My whole life I was trying to please people and make everyone happy, after a while I forgot what it meant to please myself and listen to my own needs. It is important that you do this for yourself because you are worth it.

Before I answer your question about how much I weighed when it became serious and when everyone around me was concerned I have to tell you that I never came close to what you are weighing now. Another thing is that I never skipped a period, but I guess that it all depends on

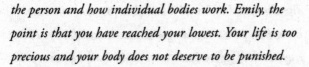

the person and how individual bodies work. Emily, the point is that you have reached your lowest. Your life is too precious and your body does not deserve to be punished.

At the time when I was too skinny, I became increasingly worried when I saw that some of my blood test results showed tremendous deficiencies in so many things. And when I was told that if I was to continue losing weight I could be faced with more serious consequences for the future, it was a wake-up call. If there is one thing I have always known it is that I want to have children one day and the thought that I might not be able to really scared me beyond anything. In my mind, I had to make an effort and force myself back to having a normal relationship with food and not see it as a threat but rather as a simple source of energy and nothing else. I was not ready to go over-board and eat a lot, but I was willing to slowly reintroduce certain things into my diet. It was not easy but I kept thinking about what I was actually putting my body through and how much I was harming myself for no reason.

You asked about symptomatic behaviour. I think it depends on the person to an extent, but thinking about food and planning for the next meal as well as wanting to know the exact composition of dishes are things that I also used to do and those are not healthy behaviours.

I have only recently seen someone specialised in eating

disorders and I now wish I had done so a long time ago. Back then, I let things drag and was in denial, so you are way ahead of where I was when it all started because you are aware and know that something is not right. Dr D is an amazing person with whom I instantly clicked ... She always used to say 'but leave your body alone, what has it done to you? Indulge yourself, trust yourself, just because you have a pain au chocolat doesn't mean you are going to raid the whole bakery!' Anyway, she was great, I think you would like her and maybe talking to her about stuff could ease things a little. It is just a suggestion and obviously entirely up to you.

Emily, I wish I could be in Geneva, I know what you are going through and even though I might talk about it as if it were easy to get out of, I know that it is not. But I believe in you and I know things will get better. Please think of yourself and cherish what you have because you are an extraordinary person with such depth and sensitivity and such tenderness, you have no reason to put yourself through any of this, no one has.

4

I was on the phone with Patrick, walking round and round in decreasing circles. I was in the garden, far from where anyone could hear. He was in New York, so far away from me it hurt. For the first time I spoke out loud what I had only recently begun to realise on paper. I needed help, and was now not only willing but eager to seek it, actively. Patrick talked with me through this inexplicable fear – of food, of pleasure, of so much more – that had now grown so huge that at times it felt hard for me to breathe. He emphasised how important it was for me to understand that I was flirting with disaster. He told me he thought the time had come for me to call the doctor Vanessa had seen, Dr D. She was a psychiatrist with an impressive record of success stories. Patrick heard my concerns about 'seeing somebody' and helped me to bend my fixed ideas by explaining that there was nothing to be ashamed of, that these people just knew how to tackle tangled knots inside when neither we, nor anyone close enough, were able to do so alone.

But above all I think I was afraid of asking my parents to take me to this shrink. I was afraid that my father would boil that option down to a pointless load of psychobabble nonsense which would only serve to confuse matters more if anything at all. I was afraid that my mother would not be able to accept that her little girl might be in need of psychiatric assistance. Patrick offered to talk to them first. I felt relieved. I passed the phone on to my parents. I waited in trepidation. And soon my anxiety was put to rest. Contrary to what I had imagined, it was only with communal relief that my relayed decision was met. My pronouncement had been met with parental approval and so, in turn, I became more resolved. In the end – and from the start – all they ever wanted was to see me smile. I wanted to smile too, for me, for them.

I walked through the hospital doors, with my father walking by my side. I took the elevator up to the psychiatric floor. Then as we walked down a corridor we passed a room to our left, where I caught the surreal glimpse of a chair laced in wires; I thought those machines belonged to a time long gone. My stomach hurt with anxiety. My heart felt tight and I began to feel faint. The stench of the hospital wrapped itself around me, permeating my clothes with the sense of something wrong, all too wrong.

We sat uncomfortably in a little corner they liked to call their waiting 'room'. It lacked discretion. There was a stack of old magazines thrown carelessly on a side table. A couple of children's books made a vague – futile – attempt at cheering the area.

Dr D was late. And time had chosen to slow its run to a casual stroll that day. The wait was one of the longest I have ever had to sit through.

Finally she appeared: middle-aged, dark-haired, piercing eyes and carrying her head high with unflinching poise. Her firm handshake and her fiery stride, as we followed her to her office, were unnerving.

Dr D sat us down and proceeded to ask me a list of questions, driving me down a road to a verdict that filled my eyes with tears of terror. Do you feel sad most of the time? Do you feel more vulnerable and fragile? Do you find it harder to draw yourself out of the cocoon that is home? Are you going out less and seeing fewer friends as days go by?

My answers were almost predetermined by the sharp tone of her voice. There was clearly a right and wrong answer and I knew which way I needed to go for her to accept what I was saying as true. It would have been just as easy to open her manual of psychiatry to the chapter on anorexia and tick the boxes myself. It all seemed rehearsed and I felt that I was being thrown into one end of a great medical medicine, subjected to codes of practices and medical jargon just to emerge out the other side, moulded into a convenient diagnosis. At that point I was no longer

Emily Halban, but just another patient she had seen that day; all of us the same as far as she was concerned. But I was in no position to question her in turn, because all her programmed questions ringed so true. I did, by now, feel sad more often than not. A sadness that had become the best of me and yet continued to feel so alien to the person I knew. I was, most definitely, more fragile, vulnerable, out of sync. I did, by this stage, find it difficult to leave home and yes, I was going out less, seeing fewer friends, amputating myself of any fun factor I once possessed.

So, *yes*.

After replying positively and politely to her stark inquisitive address, we arrived at her conclusion: 'You do know what this is all about, don't you? You do know what you've got?'

To this I shook my head, no longer able to utter a word; tears of humiliation welled up in my worried eyes.

'Yes, come on Emily, you know what this is. It isn't your fault. It is not your fault.'

Finally she voiced the verdict that had already been jotted down from the moment I entered her room, perhaps even before. All that came between was a mere preamble. It was a word I had spoken many times before, without ever really knowing what it meant. I had used it as an adjective to describe others, carelessly, without ever understanding the weight of my words. This time the decree was on me, and now the word echoed in the room: anorexia. I choked on it like a piece of food swallowed down the wrong side. It burned all the way down like the chilli that sneaked on to your fork. I feel as dizzy as a little girl spun at stomach-churning speed on a roundabout – and I had just been thrown off.

I looked at my father. I saw in his eyes so much love now dappled with deep concern, and fear. I lost myself in the watering reflection of his eyes, so soft it made me cry. His look, so intense, so intensely paternal; it was as if he was trying hard to tell me everything was going to be okay. A moment later he pulled the veil down and turned to Dr D to discuss the matter from a safe medical distance. He asked a set of practical questions and enquired about this disease she had just named with rational cool. I went silent and numb and heard very little of what they said. But I do remember Dr D saying that I was lucky because I was young, had come to her very early on in the inception of my disease and, above all, that I was seeing her out of my own volition: if I wanted to get better then the first big hurdle had already been tackled and I was on a winning track.

Dr D said that I should be hospitalised in their special unit two floors above where I would be monitored, surrounded with medical care, supervised and supported with professional attention. At this point my dad intervened, no longer as a colleague, but as a father, *my* father. He pleaded in favour of my staying at home where I would be fed with food I had always enjoyed, prepared with love no institution could claim to match, where I could continue to lead a semi-normal life while making any changes necessary to recovery; where I would be surrounded by familiar care and treated as their child rather than the new patient with a nametag but more often referred to by the number on the door of my room. Given that he is a professor in medicine and specialises in research for diabetes, my dad would be able to monitor my calorific intake and promised to follow the same guidelines as those to which I would have been forced to adhere in the clinic. The doctor was doubtful that this option would be manageable, let alone successful. She met his hopeful suggestions with a cynical sneer and brushed his optimism away saying, in effect, that she had heard all this before. But eventually she agreed, only because it was made clear to her that this dad was not stepping down. I was on probation for a limited amount of time only. A couple of weeks, no more than a month, to prove to her that this family, our team, could do it where others might have tripped.

I know my father was then asked to leave and I was left alone with Dr D. I do not remember exactly what we discussed, or what I was told, but I do remember her asking me which foods I used to enjoy had recently been barred from my list of nutritional options. I think I was reluctant to come forth and so she made a few suggestions and I eventually agreed to switching my breakfast to the new plan for that week. I was given rough guidelines for lunch and dinner too, as well as having to have a real four o'clock snack that went beyond – without excluding – my crunchy apple.

The last decision to be made – or enforced – was the inevitable use of antidepressants. I was against taking them; my parents were too. I wanted to be able to do this all by myself and believed that the colourful pills would turn me into a zombie. I was worried that I'd regress into old habits once I stopped taking them. Again, I was told that this was my disease speaking for me. Principles that I had always held were being cast aside. It was explained to me that I would still be doing the walking, only with a crutch to make it less painful and altogether more effective. I was promised that my state of mind would not alter, simply that the great moods that were currently swinging me up and down would be tempered. I eventually gave in. Again, looking back I will not criticise the use of antidepressants in certain cases and Dr D's assurances did all prove true. It is impossible to tell how much my subsequent recovery was due to their chemical help. It would not be fair to declare that my relapse was a direct consequence of my deciding to quit the medication (following strictly prescribed medical guidelines). But I do feel that their administration should be handled with more care and that so much else can be offered in the way of a crutch. And I was lucky enough, later on, to receive a different set of walking aids.

I took antidepressants for nine months from then on. I believe none of what follows should be read through the notion that any of it was achieved because of the drugs, nor that it would all have happened very differently without. They only served to turn a roller-coaster ride of ups and downs into a more tenable wiggle; the rest of my recovery was still my own.

5

I was afraid. I was confused. I was anxious. But I was willing. Although still petrified to think that I was now officially classified as anorexic, I believe I was also comforted that there was a name to my *mal-être* and that I was entitled to feel a victim. I had yet to learn exactly what the diagnosis involved, but I was fully prepared now to treat this as a medical concern. I the patient, she the specialist consultant, my parents turned doctors overnight: together we would beat this dreadful thing. It was just the medicine, four to five meals a day, that I found hard to take – and here no spoonful of sugar would do the trick.

I had been given a chance to show that I could fight the beast at home. But the threat of hospitalisation was real and I could feel the sword hanging on a thread, dangling above me with its tip softly playing with my hair.

The first time I fell anorexic, it was a hill I had to climb and the incline wasn't all too steep. I was still equipped with the naive expectation that I could beat the beast out of me – that she was my enemy, a fiercely wicked, entity of her own. That way there was a clear battle to be fought and both camps were clearly defined:

Me – my army: my parents, my brother, my sister, my best friends, my doctor

VS

Cruella – my anorexia, my illness, my affliction, my disorder

In reality all sides were mine, and the war was being fought inside me, but at the time it didn't feel that way and such graphic representations helped me keep strong in the struggle. It was not easy. I was afraid but I was also motivated by my fear. I was more flexible and willing to do what I had to do. There was a burning eagerness in me to get better. I wanted to be Dr D's best patient and for my full recovery to stand out as a beacon of hope to so many others out there. There was the same voice requiring utter perfection out of me, in sickness and in health. The little girl that wanted so much to please everyone.

Next morning, breakfast: Nutella and two slices of bread with a large glass of milk. Or, perhaps, an organic, high-quality, different but sort of similar version of Nutella and, perhaps, a pitta pouch cut open instead? This wasn't really 'cheating', it was simply bending the rules so that I might actually enjoy this food that I was suddenly, inexplicably, dreading like bad medicine. My mother came downstairs to witness the scam and soon my head was spinning with the sound of reproach and the hard accusation that *this just wouldn't do.* I felt ashamed; I felt guilt-ridden. I felt sick to the stomach with the sense of having failed, already.

I think my mother found it more difficult than anyone else to accept that I was ill. We thought it might be best if she stayed at home while my dad accompanied me to see Dr D the first time round because his was a more pragmatic approach to this sort of thing while my mother feels deeply uneasy whenever she enters a hospital. She implicitly distrusts doctors until proven wrong because she believes – and I tend to agree – that nowadays the majority are too interventionist and too far removed from nature's intended way. I think for a long time my mother blamed Dr D for giving my affliction a title, and that she believed it was in naming the thing that it then was brought about full-force. It was hard for her to accept that I needed help beyond that which she, as my mother, could possibly offer. It was, she always said, the most painful of things for a mother to see her daughter fading before her very eyes; to see the life to which she had given birth gradually dim, and over which she had no control. It was the sense of utter helplessness that caused her sleepless nights. And while my father's way of dealing with his anguish was to resort to some sort of a logical, coherent procedure with a reasonable, sensible solution, my mother's was a more emotional response. She would get angry, yell, shout, stamp her feet and slam doors. And then, moments later she would always come to me with tears in her eyes, taking me in her arms, writing notes filled with sweet consoling words and conclude, every time, with the tender simplicity of a soft spoken 'I Love You'.

When my mother encouraged me, beamed with faith in me, trusted that I would get better and stroked me with positive smiles, I felt hopeful. She would remind me of my inner strength and help me draw from it.

But when my mother got upset or angry I felt hurt and undeserving. It made me incapable of putting any good resolutions into practice and cut my appetite short. Her opinion matters to me so much. I know that she wasn't so much angry as deeply agonised and afraid. But it felt different at the time and my tendency to perceive any irritation as unreservedly directed towards me meant, inevitably, that each dart hit me straight through the heart. It took a while before my mother understood, or appreciated fully, that I was caught within the grips of a powerful disease and that it was nobody's fault – not mine, not hers, not the doctor's. It took some time, too, before she believed, really, that none of my behaviour was an assault on her. Looking back from over the fence I cannot begin to imagine what it must feel like for a mother, a parent, to have to go through such excruciating distress. I cannot blame her for her occasional outbursts of frustration towards the situation and her utter powerlessness to make matters right. It is never as simple as is written in the books, the idea that 'when the daughter stops eating it is symbolically her way of cutting the umbilical cord because she is confiscating her mother of the very basic tie they once shared which is that of the maternal feed', etc. It is all just a little more complicated and fundamentally twisted than that.

For me, one moment it was the relief of being told what to do; of being taken care of and given the routine of a newborn child. One moment it was peaceful acceptance; the hungry hatchling fed all things good and the sensation of comfort and warmth following so much bitter cold. But then the next minute it was agony at the thought of dinner to come, alarm bells ringing in a stomach all too full.

Somewhere deep inside, a little girl was trapped. And while a part of her felt safe, confined within the padded walls of control with no escape to fly away and grow, yet there was another, equally trapped, longing to break out and break free. So I was determined to do it: I was resolute in getting better before it could ever get worse. I wanted to have children one day; I wanted to go to university; I wanted to make everyone proud and show them how resilient I was. I wanted to do it myself, my way. But I also wanted my hand to be held.

Twice a week, throughout the academic year up until my exams in May, I was driven to the hospital by my mum. And sometimes there was the sense of achievement at having gained a little more weight. And sometimes that gained weight throbbed guilt against my skull. And then there was the joy at breaking good news to those who cared and the thrill of causing a hopeful smile. And then there were shoulders shrinking when the scales wouldn't play the game, and the awkward cocktail of secret relief mixed with shame for letting them all down. It was all so twisted.

There was the excitement at being encouraged and the cosiness of home-cooked food tasting sweet with a pinch of love. There were moments when it all felt right and that the end was near. But there was also pressure from all sides and the choking of being closely monitored, constantly.

And at times it gave me a headache.

At home, a typical weekday began with breakfast and my mother waking up early enough to sit down with me, for support, for supervision. After breakfast my mother would drive me to school. School was a five-minute walk away from home. It would probably have been faster to walk there, given morning traffic, than it was to take the car. But my mother drove me to make sure that there were no indispensable calories used up on a leisurely stroll. After school she was there to pick me up, invariably. On days when I had my weekly hospital appointments she would always have a snack waiting for me in a little plastic bag: three or four of my favourite biscuits with a piece of fruit and a carton of juice or a yoghurt with a banana. Otherwise we would drive back home where a similar portion of food beckoned me to eat. Then I would accompany my mum to the supermarket and decide, with her, our menu for that evening. It was more a case of my consenting to one of her suggestions than my actually calling the shots, but still it felt comforting to be entrusted, rewarded, with a certain amount of choice and made me all the more willing to make good progress.

I accepted to eat my snacks, just as I did breakfast without complaint and lunch with no objection, because they were my prescribed meals for the day and part of a set plan to which I had vowed to adhere. What I was not capable of doing was to nibble at a piece of bread, nor even an apple, outside 'eating hours', just because I happened to be hungry. The latter was greed; the former was medicine. By now though, I did enjoy much of the food I was given, when scheduled appropriately, though this was entirely dependent on the way I felt on any given day. When I felt tired, unhappy, nervous about school, then suddenly my appetite switched off and I sought refuge in the comfort of an empty stomach. I felt dizzy and light-headed when I got hungry, often just before I was due for my following daily ration. My low blood sugar levels made me irritable, touchy, easily upset. Yet on the other hand there was a fear that came with feeling satiated: when the hunger went away and my stomach felt full it was as though all the ugly feelings I had safely stored in the dark were now churning with my food and going sour. Yet another set of contradictions that left – and leaves – me confused, unable quite to make sense out of all this.

After returning home from the supermarket I would generally study in the TV room, next door to our kitchen, until summoned to dinner. Come six o'clock I would start to hear pots clanking, taps running and the tick-tick-tick of hobs switched on. Then there would always be a brief moment of panic because despite my knowing what we were having to eat, I still needed to control how it was prepared. At first it was relatively easy for me to slip into the kitchen and chit-chat away while sneaking a calculating eye at the bottle of olive oil all too dangerously placed right next to the heating pans. And I would interject just in time to make sure that the *right* amount was used with which to cook. After a while though, I was asked to stay away until I was told that everything was ready. From then on it was impossible for me to concentrate on anything other than the sounds – and smells – seeping through from the kitchen.

A similar routine applied over weekends, except that I had much more time on my hands to spend – and waste – thinking, worrying, troubling myself sick with food. I had little energy to see friends, and there were few left that I actually wanted to see, those who knew exactly what was going on and offered support without question. I would study during the day, more and more so as months went by and my exams approached, and in the evenings we would rent a film that I would watch with my parents, settled all cosy on their big comfy bed. This was not the behaviour of your average seventeen-year-old girl. But nor did I have any desire to enjoy the life an average seventeen-year-old girl might want to lead. My parents would have loved for me to go out, be sociable, see friends, have fun, and they were always delighted whenever I did agree to step outside after dark. But they were also sensitive enough not to push me beyond my limits, not to apply any more pressure than was already weighing down on my not-so-sturdy shoulders. So, for the time being, that was how my evenings on a weekend were spent.

Weekends were particularly taxing because that was when my dad took over in the kitchen. My father loves to cook. He doesn't cook a heavy meal by ordinary standards, but he does make generous use of olive oil and is not shy to add a knob of butter for taste. Ever since I fell ill, he removed the butter from our green beans and would no longer add a dollop of cream to any pea purée either. However, he would still have to use minimal amounts of olive oil in order to concoct the sort of dishes he liked to prepare. And so, come Saturday afternoon, despite knowing that I shouldn't be in the kitchen, I found myself crafting ways to lurk around there. Nosing over steaming pots, peeking scrupulously into sizzling pans and dragging out any topic of discussion with my dad to mask every inspective glance. I once looked forward to our weekend meals. There is a taste of sweet nostalgia that adds flavour to any roast chicken, saffron risotto, spaghetti with home-made tomato sauce and shepherd's pie doused in ketchup. But once I became ill my weekends were met with dread and laced with apprehension. It makes me sad. And it makes me feel guilty to think that while my father was pouring litres of love and gallons of good intentions into his food, I was losing sleep over calculations, methods of deception and half-decent excuses to override his goodwill.

One night I was called to dinner and came to the kitchen, famished, expecting a tableful of 'Emily-friendly' food. Instead, my dad had decided to cook a cheese soufflé. And then the familiar flush of panic struck and I began to feel faint – more faint. This was a weekday and I was therefore not prepared to have to handle any unpleasant culinary surprise. Soufflé should not have been on the menu that evening: it was not what I had decided with my mother at the supermarket earlier that day. Soufflé was not part of the plan – and soufflé was a hurdle I was not ready to jump yet. My grandmother was dining with us. Her presence meant that I felt less comfortable voicing my concerns, and unable to release the outburst that was boiling inside. I tried so hard to put on a brave face and reason myself into reaching inner calm. But reason chose to listen to another reasoning that night, the voice that said they were all conspiring against me, that they didn't get it, that I was fighting alone now, fighting all sides at once. My eyes began to spin and I could hear nothing other than the internal dialogue hollering in my head. I sat down next to my sister and she caught my nervous twitch. My sister was pregnant by now and there was a newfound maternal radar in her that immediately sensed my trepidation. She nudged me gently under the table with her knee, a nudge that said 'I am right here' and sought to restore confidence in me through her gentle touch. But I had already reached a point of no return.

Discreetly, she whispered, 'What's wrong?' – and there was my cue.

I stood up, rushed into the pantry and burst into desperate tears. They flowed straight out of my gut, those tears, and made my stomach hurt. My sister flew out after me and took me in her arms, quietening me down with a tender hush: no words, no questions, just a simple soothing hug. I told her what was wrong; she asked me if I would try to sit back down and taste, at least, just one mouthful, that was all. Eventually, when I was once again able to draw a deep unbroken breath, I agreed to return to the table. Having let it all out I felt tired, but relieved. Just having her by my side, if not on my side, was enough to reassure me and persuade me to head back to my plate. Meanwhile, in the kitchen, my parents knew exactly what was going on. I wish I knew what went on there while I was in the other room. I can only imagine their shared saddened looks, probably not saying much because my puzzled grand-mother was with them still. When I walked back to my chair no one asked for further explanation: I was not even harassed with a probing glance. No one was angry. Everyone wanted to make things better. That was how we managed in our house; that was how we got through these difficult times amongst others. Together, we found solu-tions and found ways to achieve appeasement at all costs. Like this, without pressure and when I was not forced, I had a spoonful of soufflé, swallowed in a rapid gulp. I didn't enjoy the taste, but I felt proud for having given it a go. And I felt loved, and hopeful too.

This was my last year of school. The year in which I was to sit my final exams, apply to university, think about the future and consider, eventually, packing my bags. It was a year of big decisions and great changes that involved putting into practice all the grand achievement I had always hoped to realise. These were the ultimate pages of a huge chapter in my life and ahead of me were blank slates waiting to be filled with notable things. I was determined not to allow anorexia to get in the way of it all. I knew too well how important it was for me to feel accomplished – how important it was for the sake of my no longer suffering from this ill.

I wrote to Vanessa at the time:

To Vanessa 26 September 2000 (aged 17)

It's horrible, on the one hand I want so much to get better – to get well, but on the other hand whenever anyone congratulates me for having eaten well it freaks me out because what I hear is, 'wow you have eaten so much' and where I go with that is fear.

School starting isn't a great help, and yet it is … It puts pressure on me, which I honestly could do without at the moment, but it also allows me to get out of the house and to realise that I have no time to spare because this year is going to go by so quickly and it is too important for me to mess it up. I have kind of lost interest in many so-called friends who don't seem to care, understand or even try to understand; who simply look and most probably talk. Let them talk.

Somewhere deep down I was afraid. So frightened of leaving home, terrified at the thought of growing up, and anxious that I would not be good enough nor even anywhere near. I remember skimming through old family photo albums and shedding tears over snaps of me as a little girl, laughing, with a constant twinkle in my eye.

My mother has kept these albums neatly aligned on a bookshelf, all in chronological order, filled with memories spanning back to the very first shots we ever took, promises that the stories of our lives are captured in time no matter how far the clock continues to tick ahead. And yet, far from reassured I only felt more sad, more troubled, more scared. They were feelings, in fact, that had started already at the time my mum had caught the blues and that had continued to creep into my veins in stronger doses ever since. By now they were acutely painful but I was not equipped with any psychological tools necessary to deal with them. And Dr D was too busy worrying about my weight, unable to see that there was a far greater weight that I was under. So, lost in a whirlwind of uncertainty riddled with fear, the only way I found to keep hold of the bridle was to rein in on my food.

Essentially, although she was a psychiatrist and might have been expected to talk to me about what was going on in my head, Dr D's approach seemed driven almost entirely by a forceful focus on my food. She would weigh me every time I was to see her, which was scheduled for twice a week to start. We barely had time to talk about anything else. Our sessions always started, after the customary stiff shake of my hand, with my stripping down to pants and bra and stepping on the scales. In the elevator going up to her floor I would think through the meals and snacks I had eaten since I had last seen her and wonder, half hoping, half dreading, whether I had eaten enough to tip the balance. It was a matter of grams at this stage: every gram lost marked a real defeat and pushed me that much closer to being shoved into a room on their hospital ward. When the scales tilted back Dr D would let out a sigh of regret that stabbed straight at my heart. At the same time, she also reminded me in a semi-victorious tone that 'it wasn't my fault; that this disease was very resilient', the underlying meaning being that I needed help beyond what I was currently receiving at home, as she had predicted from the first. I felt ashamed, embarrassed almost, that I was not up to her standards, not managing the challenge she had put forth. But above all it was always the disgrace of disappointing my parents who were pouring so much of themselves on to me, my recovery. I couldn't deal with disappointment, because along with disappointment there came guilt, and a deep sense of unworthiness – and both, in turn, were anorexia's favourite fodder. I know this now: back then instead it all came in a tangled knot in my stomach and a knotty lump in my throat. But Dr D continued to concentrate only on the physical manifestation of my ills.

There were weeks when my weight remained the same; then she would just state the obvious in repeating that while at least I hadn't lost, really the aim here was to gain at serious speed, and that didn't seem to be happening, did it?

And then there were, more and more, times when I did put on weight, anywhere between 100g to 1kg in one week. Those days she was always quick to cool down my excitement and deflate any momentary pride in reminding me that there was still a long way to go and that I couldn't rest on this one battle to win the war. There were never any words of encouragement. I understand that she needed to keep me in check. I know that she was trying to step ahead of Cruella who would inevitably try to suggest to me, as soon as I walked out the door, that I had failed. But actually, unlike the stereotypes with which I had indiscriminately been labelled, I really did want to get better and I was fighting with all the strength I could summon. I always went to the loo *before* stepping on the scales so that I could be sure that the number displayed was absolutely real, contrary to what stories I have heard of other patients drinking gallons of water in order to trick the scales. Even then, there should have been an allowance reserved for fluctuating levels of fluid retention, especially given that I was forbidden from any exercise at that stage. It should have been the general direction of the curve that we focused on, not the minor vacillations in between unless they really amounted to something of significant concern. Instead, Dr D's approach was unequivocally laced with criticism and reproach. And it made me feel even more worthless than I already felt. Yet she had such a great record of success stories and so many people had said so much good about her that I assumed this just was the way these things worked. And I was careful only to relate any odd glimpse of a softer, more heartening side of her to my parents because I knew how much they wanted, needed, to hear positive things. And I, in turn, wanted to protect them. And I, in turn, wanted to please and make them smile.

Dr D did not believe in wholegrain foods and vegetarian alternatives. She was convinced that these were only crafty tools that I used to deviously manipulate everyone around me. And if I had been brought up on such foods, then that was part of the problem that needed to be addressed. In retrospect I understand that she was only trying to encourage – or push – me to broaden my comfort zone and break down barriers of rigid behaviour. I am sure she had met all too many times with the scheming kind of patient. But I was not like that. I had accepted to see her on my own volition. I had always been honest with my parents and was genuinely unaware of the grim picture I was painting for my future. I agree that there is a level of flexibility that is crucial to instil; anorexia is a disease that stiffens you inside out and to the bone.

But I have learned since then that there are other ways of handling such concerns; these involve building up a mutual trust where safety nets are lowered gradually before they can be altogether removed. Since then every nutritionist I have met would agree that preferring wholemeal bread – wholegrains of any sort – soya products or other meat substitutes, olive oil, fresh fruit and vegetables to a diet based on refined carbohydrates and hydrogenated or saturated fats is neither unhealthy nor deceitful. There is a fine line and it is sometimes difficult to discern; but it is there and great care should be taken to define it.

6

At school, that year, I felt increasingly alienated from my childhood friends, their glances, the whispers, that itching feeling of being misunderstood. I had always been 'popular': with many friends, confident, sociable, had boyfriends, enjoyed going out, make-up, dancing, laughing, having a good *time* – everything a girl my age could wish for, I had. I was in the same school from nursery until my final year, fourteen years a tightly knit class growing up side by side, my extended family. I loved school. I loved to learn. I loved my friends and I missed it all every summer. It was something out of a cheesy Hollywood soap. I was lucky.

There was one year, though, that I chose to spend in a different school. Having been at the same International (private) school all my life, I wanted a taste of something different and to see what the Swiss national educational system was like. So it was that, in tenth grade – *before* my mother's depression, *before* the fashion show, *before* any of that – I moved away from my sanctuary. There, I felt unsettled. It never felt quite right. My old school was a very special environment with over a hundred nationalities all offering a different flavour to the system; it was open minded and pushed its students to be above all creative, inventive, proactive. And instead, in this new school, I was stuck in archaic didactic methods of learning off by heart, reciting, regurgitating formulas set in stone. The students fit to this mould, and I did not.

I had started to date a boy the summer before going to Swiss school; he attended that place too so I was all the more excited, at first, that I would be nearer to him. But I broke up with him towards the beginning of term – which struck his pride in ways I could not have foreseen. Aged fifteen this was heart-break high and should never have taken the proportions it did. I was struck recently to find this diary entry:

25 March 1998 (aged 14)

Gerard tells everyone I'm a reject, a bitch, that I kiss badly, that I have nothing other than tits to please … Basically, Gerard is right, I am a reject, always alone now at breaks etc. So I'm working hard so that at least I get good grades!

This proves that my real friends are at Ecolint (my former school)! God, it's when you've lost what you love that you realise how much you loved it. These days I'm not well. I hate feeling this way, and I feel so selfish, my problems are so minor compared to those of so many other people. But I'm doing my best not to show how I feel; I pretend I'm fine.

These lines send a chill down my spine because I begin to see how far back I actually need to go to spot the point (if there ever is *one* point) at which I became punctured with fear, guilt, shame, and an utter sense of worthlessness. When the girl who 'had it all' and never stopped to hesitate suddenly found herself stumbling upon a lack of self-confidence and anxious insecurities.

Changing schools caused me to put myself in question. I felt distanced from the person I knew myself to be and so remote from everyone else around. Surely I would have to learn to adapt to new settings in life, but this one was altogether so incongruous with my way of thinking that I felt out of place, both inside and out.

Then I went back to Ecolint and I never really fell back into the swing of things. One year later and my feelings were already beginning to forecast the squall that was to come.

13 January1999 (aged 15)

*I thought that coming back to my old school would make
me feel myself again. That I would have no difficulties
feeling secure. Obviously my hopes were illusions. Not only
do I not feel secure, I most of all feel stupid. Everyone is
suddenly so grade-conscious. I once wasn't, now I want the
tops, and I don't think I'm capable of that. I don't know if
I'm intelligent enough to go to Oxford, even less to get any
of my poems published. I feel like I constantly need to prove
my intelligence. At the same time I don't want to be a little
nerd, a person who got somewhere just as anybody could, by
working hard and repeating everything like an anaesthetised
parrot. That is something admirable because it demands a
certain amount of will and concentration. But I would just
like people to be maybe not astonished, but somewhat
touched by my intelligence. By saying this I am not
implying that I do have good brains, but simply that I
would love to be spoken of as an intelligent girl.*

*Where am I headed? Where is all of this ending? And
above all, will anyone remember me?*

*I am so afraid of the future. The more I think of it, the
more I have flashbacks of being a very little girl. And I feel
so worried.*

It's just that there is so much to learn out there and I am
beginning to feel more and more like a little snowflake,
ephemeral, amidst millions of others in a gigantic
atmosphere.

Meanwhile, now, at school, final exams pending, I had a new period of readjustment to manage. These people knew me too well for me to be able to hide. They had, in fact, been the first to point out that I was heading in the wrong direction, before my parents even came to the same conclusion. I am an honest person. I believe you can rarely go wrong when being sincere, and the same applies to the way I handled anorexia. From the moment I was presented with the disease, I never tried to deny it. I was not secretive and always happy, eager even, to talk about what was going on and try to explain things as best I could. My friends, those who were genuinely concerned, deserved an update. And I needed to silence any rumours that could be heard so loud and clear in the quiet that filled a room whenever I walked in. So much had happened over the summer and while on the one hand I wanted everyone to know that I was taking care of myself – or being taken care of – at the same time I found it difficult to be surrounded by anyone who didn't really understand what was going on, and very few possibly could. So I made one round of explanations to hush the ugly gossip, and then I kept inside the safe circle of those who didn't need any justification of mine. Olivia was one who knew me beyond words. Olivia, my sister-soulmate who always stood by my side.

Lunchtime was hardest. Our school cafeteria was divided in two by pillars and each section had its own self-service queue – both sides serving the same food. Our year always sat on the right-hand side, towards the back and near the windows. Younger classes tended to stick to the left. I migrated that way too. Olivia was my very best friend and the only friend I could stomach sitting by my side as I ate. It wasn't just that I would 'tolerate' her presence, but more that while I could not deal with being amongst glaring crowds, yet I was also somehow utterly unable to eat alone. Listening to the little girl I was beginning to hear inside, I needed a helping hand; someone to offer implicit support and encouragement, without judgement, without saying a word, just being my friend. And that is what Olivia did. Every day she met me in the queue and kept me company while I ate. Sometimes we chose the same, other days she preferred a different dish. It didn't matter. I felt reassured to have her eating there with me. I was calmed to feel her silently care; it felt safe to be shielded by her friendship.

Perfect

One day, one day only, I walked to meet Olivia and she wasn't there. Panic struck me so deep as I turned round and round in circles, peering over happy smiling faces, and pushed my way through hungry students, hoping to catch sight of her through what was turning into an overwhelming crowd. I needed my food, but I could not eat it all by myself. My blood sugar levels were reaching a hazardous low. I lacked the strength to take the unexpected in my stride. The plan was that we met every day, same place, same time. That was the plan and if she couldn't stick to it she had to let me know in advance so I could make another plan instead, or prepare myself, at least, for the prospect of being on my own. I felt let down. I felt unsafe. I began to feel confused, and afraid. My appetite fled and I held on tight to hunger in the lonely hole that encaged me all around. Finally she answered her mobile and casually apologised; she had been caught up in town with friends, having had a free period just before lunch. She had no idea that her absence could have created such panic in me. She was sorry and could hop on a bus to meet me if I really wanted. Of course I really wanted her to come. But it would have been unfair of me to make such needy demands. I knew that much, though the remainder of my level-headed reasoning had escaped from me. I was in tears, reduced to a disadvantaged little girl – and that, in turn, felt even more belittling.

Any other seventeen-year-old girl might have been pissed off, annoyed, momentarily outraged at having been 'dumped' at the last minute. A regular seventeen-year-old girl might also have jumped on a bus to meet all her friends in town. Otherwise, perhaps, she would have found another group of friends to sit down with that day. Failing that, a normal seventeen-year-old girl would, ultimately, not have been quite so terrified at the thought of eating alone, just this once. And yet here was I, shaking like a kitten thrown into a pool, frightened and sad. Had I been given warning, I could have set my mind to programming an alternative plan. I could then have pictured what I was going to eat, where I might like to sit, alone, and adjusted to the new scenario in time for lunch. How hard it must have been for Olivia – for anyone – to comprehend; I couldn't understand it myself. Anorexia is a stealer of spontaneity; after an initial brainwash, she then retrains the mind to think only in terms of fixed plans and set strategies.

In recovery, routine becomes as important as it is to a newborn baby. It is essential that a strict timetable be adhered to and agreed agendas observed. This is a way of playing in to the disease, as it were, and playing along with the need for everything to be predetermined, while drawing up a new schedule, one based on recuperating a Life.

From then on Olivia, sensitive to my need for everything

to be set in advance, in stone, gave me notice on days when she would not be able to meet her engagement. On those days my mum would come to have lunch with me. I liked that too. That same feeling of security, of being looked after without being judged. There was a restaurant in town that served a variety of fresh salads, hot food and fruit of choice, all with a selection of sauces served on the side, all self-service. Once in a while my mum would meet me at the school gate and whisk me away for a midday break. This was effectively my only other hub of 'happy' food where I felt comfortable outside school and home. It allowed me to choose – and verify – what I wanted to go on my plate (with my mother's helping hand). There was no pressure and no one there to judge. For a long time after, I found it hard to go back there because it harked back to too many painful memories. I wonder if I could today.

But on the whole restaurants were a non-event. It was that I would inevitably be shaken from a set timely routine. It was also the anguish of having to skim through an entire menu when hungry and make decisions while ultimately having no real control over the way in which my food would be prepared, not portion sizes, nor quality; nothing. There was the risk that pots were not properly scrubbed before being employed to cook my food, pots that might have come into contact with butter, cream, oil or lard. There was only so much a waiter could understand and I was always convinced that there would be a great big conspiracy to hide unwanted fat somewhere on my plate and disregard my pleas to keep it free from dangerous stuff. So I developed infallible techniques for supreme inspection. The first step was to check for any tell-tale glistening. The second was carefully to touch the food and rub my fingers for that oily feel. Then, if I still suspected evil, I would douse my food in vinegar, allowing it to soak through the food and leak on to the edges of my plate, and I would scrutinise that excess liquid to see whether there were any floating particles.

I sent my food back more than once. I remember one particular occasion when I was with my parents in one of my favourite restaurants and ordered a side dish of spinach. It came, it glistened, it felt all too slippery and ultimately there were elements of grease swimming in my vinegar. Three times the waiter rushed back and forth between our table and the kitchens, promising that the chef had sworn he had cooked the spinach in water. But I remained disbelieving. Finally, the kitchens accepted that, perhaps, they might have used a pan in which they may previously have used a touch of oil. Spinach, thereafter, was a side dish I would not order.

I felt safer going to restaurants with my parents because they would protect me and ensure that my requests were respected, fully. They knew how big a step it was for me to accept to go out and recognised that while it was important for me to blow a great big breath of confidence into my comfort zone, it was also essential not to pull so hard on the band that it would snap back into my face with violent force. They were so good in recognising my limits, encouraging my steps forward and providing the padding necessary for me to be willing to leap once in a while. So much so that in order to ensure our meals out remained a pleasing, peaceful, stress-free event my father came to telling waiters that I had a medical condition that meant that I simply could not process *any* fat of *any* sort and that it was therefore of *utmost* importance that my dish arrive exactly as it had been asked for.

I would skim through the menus of most restaurants I walked past to pre-empt the possibility of ever being taken there and to make my own mental list of eating places that met basic criteria: enough salads that were not filled with unwanted nasties; a good number of side dishes I could order with 'no butter, no oil, pure and simple please, thank you very much'. It was, simply put, the lack of control that I could not master and the fear of not being able to control that I could not dominate. And yet the truth is that control had long since been sneaked away from me. Cruella is supremely twisted and shrewd.

7

My progression advanced at astonishingly rapid pace. I was treated with the medicine of love and fuelled by the faith of my parents that I would get better. I was determined to make true their trust in me. In addition, I had my exams coming up and I knew I must be strong enough, both mentally *and* physically in order to sit them. And I was so desperate to fight what I perceived as being the enemy within. I had not befriended Cruella; I was no accomplice of hers. I know that it can often spiral into such sordid, perverse affairs, like a Stockholm syndrome of the mind, the hostage developing signs of loyalty to the hostage-taker, anorexia. But at this point in my life I was looking only to escape.

18 January 2001 (aged 17)

Good news: I gained another 500g!
   Bad news: yesterday I came home from school and was

going to have a snack. I went to the kitchen and poured some cereal into a bowl. Maman sat down with me because she too was having some cereal and this absolutely infuriated me. Because I wanted to put one mini-millilitre of milk and then dilute it with water but I wasn't about to do that in her presence or she would have flipped – and not without reason. So I made myself an orange juice and drank it VERY slowly, waiting for her to be done. I had to make such an effort of self-control not to get angry, snap or lose it altogether. I was mad because my mother was there. But I was angry most of all because Cruella was there too.

There are a number of little victories that stand out proudly with a brightly coloured flag. They were when I managed to reintroduce an ingredient or dish I always used to relish. Culinary delights I had taught myself to enjoy only through a highly developed olfactory aromatic taste. They came and went, these brief glimpses of light, but every time they sparkled a little more bright, and with time they became easier to ignite.

Perfect

9 February 2001

My first (whole!) pizza – without cheating, without compensating.

That week I was supposed to have two slices of bread (as dictated by Dr D) with Nutella and a glass of orange juice for a snack (twice) – and to have a pizza with salad one day. The idea was for me to reintroduce, little by little, all the things that I would have eaten in the past. In fact, Dr D wanted me to surpass myself and *expand* that list even further to being able to eat anything without going red, purple and blue in the face. The prospect of reaching beyond the limits of what I once enjoyed was one too daunting for now, but I was willing to make the first step in returning to foods I used to choose. That much I could do.

I hadn't had a pizza in seven months.

When I told my parents about the pizza they were very pleased but suggested why not have a 'top-quality pizza' rather than greasy muck that I would hate. They were just trying to help make it easier for me, I know, and reassure me in the challenge that was set. And they were right, really: there was no reason why I should force down a wedge of nastiness under any circumstances, but it's not like I was ever going to do that anyway. I agreed with them but the truth is that deep (*deep*) down I think in a way the whole purpose of that exercise was precisely to step outside my comfort zone and reach a place where I would be able to accept a night out with friends in some shabby pizzeria and eat the thing with everyone else – without fear. Then again, I preferred to treat myself at that stage. Yes, I think I deserved a treat.

So it was carefully planned and I knew exactly where I wanted to have my first pizza in months. It would be with Olivia and in a place where they cooked their pizzas in a wood-fired oven (no greasy pans) and where the crust was very fine. But the point is that I stood by my plan, felt the prickle of fear – and then that tingle of satisfaction. It was like the child learning how to walk for the very first time, a little wobbly at first, then ambling happily along – soon to break into a run! It tasted good, it felt good, it slipped down okay and I too was okay! And I didn't suddenly feel the urge to gulp down another three along with a side order of garlic bread and a whole chocolate cake to finish. I did not lose control. My hunger stopped when it was satisfied. Satisfied.

11 February 2001

I had the pizza on Friday, I was SOOOO proud – it was good too! And then, for the first time (in a VERY long time) I was watching TV the other day and my mum had a bowl of nuts and raisins sitting on the table and I had some

raisins, out of the blue, just like that, because I felt like it! I
haven't 'munched' at an 'unusual time' (i.e. unplanned; not
breakfast, lunch, prescribed snack or dinner time) for an
eternity. I won't hide that I had walked a little more than
usual that afternoon and that I therefore felt reassured that
it was okay, and that I also reasoned with myself that
raisins are a 'healthy' food (I may not have grabbed a fun-
sized Snickers). But still, I would never have allowed myself
such an indulgence before. So, actually, this is big.

23 February 2001

The day my sister gave birth.

That is one of few key moments I can pin down as so-called
'turning points'. There is another motivation that always
dragged me forward whenever I felt myself slipping. That
is the burning desire to have children one day – and the
fear that I might not should this thing drag on too long.
When my sister announced that she was pregnant there
were tears of utter happiness mixed with other overwhelming emotions. She was due a few weeks before my
Baccalaureate exams. My flight was booked for the day
before she was expected to deliver. I arrived late that
evening. We all dined together. My parents went back to

their hotel room and I stayed to sleep at my sister's house. We all went to bed. The next thing I knew I had my sister flying past me to the bathroom, laughing with the giggle of a little girl; her waters had broken and it was time to go! It was 3 a.m.

I leaped out of bed, threw on my customary tracksuit with a jumper to keep me warm. I flew downstairs and into the kitchen where my brother-in-law was making toast in anticipation of a long day ahead. He offered me a slice. Normally I would have declined the recommendation that I have a piece of bread smeared with butter and layered with honey in the middle of the night, well ahead of calculations for the day to come and far beyond yesterday's already totalled count. But now I grabbed a wedge, popped it into the toaster, spread it with all things good and scoffed it down to the final crumb. Cruella had no space to squeeze herself through such a momentous occasion. The bigger picture was far too tangible for her to distort it with her twisted ways. It was a victory unforeseen and this time I was waging war. It felt thrilling and I was filled with the bubbling sensation of newborn hope.

Two days after my niece's birth I reached an all-important landmark in my resurgence: fitting my first pair of jeans in six months. I had a closet full of tracksuits and other such loose trousers in that period of time: comfy outfits with an elastic tie that somehow managed to grip on to the sorry excuse I had for a waist. But also comfy clothes that made me feel snug, cosy, safe; and that allowed me to eat 'freely' without then feeling any unpleasant tightness nor having to undo buttons; clothes that would not provoke me with frightening alarm when they suddenly no longer fit. I was so proud that day, the day I agreed to try on a pair of jeans and that they didn't make me look like I was going fishing. Before that I had always refused because I knew that only the children's section might cater for my form, and I was conscious not to set myself up for a full-blown freak-out effect the day I eventually outgrew a size 10 (year-old's) dress. Slipping on that pair of jeans, and walking out of the changing room to flaunt my still-not-so-big-but-no-longer-shocking waistline with a twirl was a moment I will never forget. Perhaps, in fact, the greatest achievement lay in the thrill itself; that I was genuinely happy to have reached a shape for jeans.

27 March 2001

My first slice of apple tart – no tricks, no compensation.

Apple tart: a favourite 'forbidden' food of finger-licking delight. One that filled me with fear but to which I also looked forward, secretly. Cruella was losing her power over me by now. I remember the day so clearly. Sunshine fore-cast for an afternoon of bright hopeful things. It was a carefully selected slice in a specially chosen bakery; the best in town. I walked in and the naughty pleasure of toffee-sweet smells filled me with enchantment. There were different kinds of pastry from which to choose. I chose the one that looked the least grease-laden. But it was still a real, unadulterated, slice of apple tart, and they were generous with their portions too. I stepped out into the summer sun and sat myself by a fountain. Comfortably installed, I opened my parcel delicately, slowly, and took a bite. As the apple melted softly on my tongue, wrapped in its pastry, it all burst with the essence of pleasure. And I allowed myself to taste the pleasure too.

Because this is the point. Contrary to one of many popular beliefs, anorexia is not about not being hungry; it is about controlling hunger and the sense of safety that comes with feeling in complete domination of life because we are effectively mastering the one key element that ensures our very existence. And the more hungry we become, the tighter that feeling of control. Appetite too is dominated by the fear of losing control over a craving growing stronger every day. And our mind learns ways to trick us into believing that we can get fuel off the thought of food and take pleasure, should we ever deserve such enjoyment, in the smell that bubbling pots and frying pans let loose around a home. Perhaps, in a moment of weakness, we will give in to temptation and venture to taste a mouth-watering treat. But then there were also ways to taste without having to swallow – spitting when no one is around to look, chewing enough for every bud to salivate and savour, then spewing the splodge into the bin. That developed later – and it was a trait I soon gave up when I was hit with dread that this was a stepping stone towards tripping into bulimia. I never made myself sick – not least because I don't know how!

I admit to trying once, making myself sick, but I never managed to see it through. And I never tried again, not least because I know that should I ever have found that tickly spot that empties the stomach so it never feels full I would have been tempted to try that again and again and once more after that – until I found myself hooked. It was like the lure of a drug that promises an immeasurable life. 'Emptiness' was the addiction that I needed to quit, for good.

8

There comes a point in losing weight when nature's ordinary course is curtailed. Our bodies are so finely tuned that if we are in no physical state to bear a child, our reproductive system will automatically shut down until we are fit once more to procreate. In other words, the summer I dropped too many kilos my period stopped and throughout my anorexia it would not return. For me, there was a driving fear factor here that helped push me forward whenever I was inclined to slip back. I wanted so much to have a family one day that I could not stand to think that I might be jeopardising that dream. When my sister gave birth, it was one of the most moving moments in my life – and seeing her hold that baby in her arms stirred me deeply. For me, the ultimate goal was for my period to return; that would be my body's natural way of saying that I could rest assured.

It was the month of April, just before the very end of school. Nine months had gone by since the official launch of my battle against anorexia, and I was winning. I had gained ten kilos, had reached a near-acceptable shape, and I was more and more compliant to those things that would make me heal. Every weekend now, I would meet up with Olivia and another friend, Michael, to study together in a public library. Getting out of the house and spending time away from home with friends; this was what I now wanted to do. I started to fancy Michael and remember vividly peering over my books to steal an undetected stare at him for as long as I could while he sat there assiduously taking notes. I wanted to have fun and had regained the confidence to take a jump. The conversations in my head had hushed to such an imperceptible whisper that I could finally begin to take notice once more of others around.

We were all three in the library when I felt an unfamiliar trickle send warm vibrations through my spine. Every day, every time I went to the bathroom it was always with the longing for a spot of electrifying red. This time, however, I was all too immersed in revision – or entertaining my crush – for me to think of anything else. I just needed the loo. So I got up and walked silently out to the hall. I can still hear the echoing sound of the toilet doors slamming shut behind me and I can see myself casually sitting on the loo seat, still concentrating on moments that defined the Cold War, whilst unbeknown to me was that here would be a defining point of my own. I will never forget dashing breathless on to the street to make a million phone calls and spread the word: my period was back! *I* was back! That was the ultimate hurdle and I had cleared it, flying high. Now I could begin to feel a woman once more. I was *not* afraid of the underlying implications, that it meant I had in fact put on a substantial amount of weight; that there was now a future I had to face; that I must accept everything that came with growing up and assume the responsibilities involved. It was all really exciting, nothing more.

I sat my exams and passed with top marks. I graduated with every honour on the table and held my head up high with a deftly rolled diploma in my hand. Michael and I fell head over heels. That summer we got together, like two joyful teenagers and a thousand butterflies in between. I was accepted to Oxford and had a summer of utter freedom set before me. No constrictions, obligations, limitations nor constraints. And a driving licence too. We all went to Italy and I was feeling light, though not light-headed.

I felt loved, loving and lucky.

I slowly cut down on the pills. This made me feel a little dizzy at first. My head pounded heavily and the occasional white speck blurred my vision. It made me realise the potency of that sweet-shaped drug. And I was happy to be moving on to sweeter things.

By the end of summer, one year on, everything seemed back to 'normal'. I was headed for Oxford despite Dr D's feeling that I was not quite ready just yet. I refused to heed her pessimism; I had had enough of that. By the time I was due to fly from the nest it felt like I was doing so with a pair of brand-new wings. We all were now focusing on my smile that had returned. I felt 'fine'. All was 'fine'. There was, perhaps, a scar somewhere but it was not obvious. Not to anyone who chose to look elsewhere. And we all did.

9

I arrived at university conscious, somewhere, of the fact that although my physical appearance may not have revealed any worrying condition, still mine were wounded wings and my flight away from home – my *nest* – was bound to be a more challenging journey than most of my peers were experiencing with utter glee.

I arrived at university and I was doing well; I was making friends; I was joining societies and acting in a play. And yet …

I arrived at university and I felt afraid.

I arrived at university and I wanted to go home.

I arrived at university and I wanted to be a little girl.

I arrived at university and Cruella came to seduce me once more with her comforting ways and reassuring voice. And she reminded me what to do at times when everything around feels strange and unknown. I tasted the luscious flavour of hunger once more. Soon I was never alone; always accompanied by her whispers. And then she was me and I was her shadow as we pranced side by side holding hands, tightly gripped.

Dr D allowed me to go to university on the condition that I should continue to be weighed and monitored by a doctor in Oxford. I remember the stale smell in the doctor's waiting room, surrounded by crying babies and white-faced mothers with very little light shining through their tired eyes; a receptionist, so bored, calling out our names through a boxed opening in the wall. I know I always had tears in my eyes when speaking to that doctor. I know my updates were always recounted with a choke. And yet she saw nothing. I cannot blame her for it; I might have been homesick, it could have been a natural difficulty to adjust that was bound to fade within a couple of months. I couldn't bring myself to spell out that I needed help because that was giving in and giving in meant defeat, and I didn't do defeat. But the hints weren't heard and soon I stopped going. I explained to my parents that the doctor and I just didn't get along. I projected a happy face through my voice and sent comfort down the phone. They accepted, confident that I was okay.

We had a few 'welfare officers' in college, one of whom was named Emma; she was in the year above ours and I had spotted her as seeming particularly gentle and kind. More than once I had seen her walking by and thought it might be a good idea to have a chat. Just to talk to someone my age, but not in my immediate group of friends, and whose position suggested she was well placed to understand. I was in the library one afternoon, feeling blue. My throat felt tight; my stomach ached with homesickness. Emma was sitting, alone, at a desk in a corner, making notes. Everyone was hushed and all faces were hidden behind stacks of books. I tiptoed towards her and kneeled by her side, whispering what might have been harder to say out loud. She looked at me with intensely compassionate eyes and suggested that we go and have a cup of tea in her room. There, she offered me so wide a selection of herbal infusions that it equalled none other than my own. She had biscuits on display, but also a bowl filled with fruit and she was careful to make clear I was welcome to help myself without shoving anything uncomfortable my way. She clearly knew what she was doing – or was it that she could actually relate to me, beyond her responsibility?

As we chatted it soon became clear that we were on the same page. She too tended to channel any emotional overload through a need to control her food. Suddenly we were sisters and the dynamic had changed from seeking consolation to sharing common support. And finally we made a pact: that together we would engage in battle against the brute and build a strong offensive, cheering each other on. It felt so good to be understood beyond words. I had found more than a friend. Compassion had turned to empathy, and it was mutual. Nothing can compare with knowing that you are not alone in your shadowy patch, no matter how divergent the leading paths might have been to get there and regardless, even, of differing reactions in the shade. The point is just that there is no longer the need for explanations, justifications, rationalisations. It is so important to feel valued without question.

Emma was babysitting the following week and we decided to make that night the launching date of our crusade. I would join her and we would order pizza. What could be so frightening about a pizza? Everyone did it all the time, eating pizza. If they could do it so could we – and if they enjoyed it so would we. We sat by the telephone with the restaurant's number staring at us on the table; there was a pink elephant in the room but we chose not to take notice. Perhaps we could share? Or was that cheating? No, they were smallish, those pizzas, and we would each have our own. So we ordered and waited patiently till it was time to pick them up. I had already done the whole pizza thing once before, and yet I could feel myself stalling. Emma had to stay at home with the children so I went out to fetch our trophies. Once we put the little ones to sleep we sat ourselves down, lifted the lids, allowed the wicked smells to escape from their parcel and prod us with a cheesy tang. Emma was inspiring in her poise, as slowly she ate one slice after the other without so much as a flinch. There was no music on and we could hear each other chew. But I was not chewing much and every mouthful was swallowed with a painful gulp trying hard to choke back the tears. I couldn't do it. The pizza had not been cooked by wood-fire but in a pan; that was unexpected. Its crust was so much thicker than what I had seen in my mind. I felt so ashamed, angry at myself and guilty that I had also dragged Emma down in my defeat. But she pulled me back on my feet and together we decided it wasn't over till it was over. So, once the babysitting was over and we were free to go, we went out to another eating place next door, where their crust was thin despite the pizzas being double in size, and where they were made without a pan, over fire, the dough simply dusted with a bit of extra flour. We were in the company of others, cutlery clinking against emptied plates, smiling happy people, laughter all diluting the fear. We had our pizza and ate it. And walked out feeling proud, all the more proud at having picked ourselves up. But not without a graze. And when I went to bed that night the scrapes began to sting.

The thing about eating disorders as compared to any other 'addictive' or 'compulsive' personalities is that there is this sordid sort of fatal attraction and an innate sense of competitiveness. But all this makes it tricky for two sufferers to shoulder each other forward. On the one hand there is nothing that feels more comforting and no compassion that can equate to that sense of being understood, beyond words, on the same level of experience. On the other hand there is the danger that suddenly you are no longer lending sympathetic support, not even sharing similar accounts, but rather swapping stories, trading sick attributes, borrowing each other's shoes. And that is not okay.

I returned home for Christmas and went to see Dr D at the hospital; a simple check-up as promised before going off against her will. A simple check-up turned quickly into familiar threats of checking me in and suddenly it was difficult to swallow.

I would not be going back to Oxford the following term. I could stay at home provided I proved capable of switching the digits on her weighing machine to a figure she had in mind. I would visit her, at the hospital, twice a week. But I would also fly over to Oxford once a fortnight to hand in essays and sit a double tutorial because although I may be physically frail, still it was my sense of self-worth that would ultimately tip the scales and that meant carrying on with my studies.

I now had to tell my friends. I couldn't leave without any explanation and nor did I want to make space for wrongful speculation. I had always been open about my anorexia in the past. *My* anorexia, is that already what she had become?

Perfect

One by one I sat in individual rooms and took anxious looks through to considerate expressions of concern. And so, by saying things as they were and trying to make as much sense of it all as I possibly could, I was building nests of friendship woven with an honesty that would subsist to any storm. I had opened my arms out wide and so they all did the same. It was so much easier that way.

But I was incapable of hearing my own words of wisdom.

We wrote emails to each other all through my time back home. I wanted them to know all about what I was going through so that when I returned there would be no pink elephant sitting in the middle of the room and no wide gulf created between us because so much had happened since. There was one, long, email I sent to Sam. Sam had recently become one of my closest friends and yet I hadn't had the time to talk him through the situation before I left. I felt I owed him an explanation and it became a template for so many letters after that.

To Sam, 27 February 2002 (aged 18)

Where to begin? I guess it must be difficult to perceive what is going on in my mind and why I don't just snap out of whatever it is that impedes upon my operating properly.

I myself cannot quite understand what is going on up there – it has come to a point whereby I analyse myself with utter coherence on a theoretical level, but just miss the bus every time it comes around to pick me up and push theory into action. Anorexia is an illness labelled with such a plethora of preconceived, misguided stigmas. Notably, it is inexorably linked with a concept of superficiality and affectedness, both of which I hope you will never come to tag me with, and both of which are so mistaken in any case.

It is hard to imagine what goes on inside what seems to be a perfectly functional mind ... well, the truth remains that far from being tightly screwed on, this head of mine is actually pretty screwed up right now!

I am not in denial of my state (contrary to what seems generally to be a common factor in this disease), but I am neglectful of myself. It is impossible to say where or when it all began, but at one point in my perfectly happy and healthy life I slipped the slender slope of confidence and headed a dangerous trail down to a world of rigorous control, strict obedience and severe punishment. I was trapped in thinking I was master of the game when in fact I am a mere rookie. Cruella (the twisted spirit that has hand-cuffed my appetite for life – but not for a lifetime) will not let me be. She takes over my senses and manages my existence in sly persuasion that I do not deserve to let go, have fun, seize the day with all its fine opportunities and precious gifts. I do realise that I am too thin, at least I think I do, and that almost makes things harder because it is all so upside-down. When it comes to reaching targets though, things are not as simple as the resolutions I had taken tend to suggest. For so long now (exactly how long and why I cannot say for sure), I have excluded from my diet virtually all 'fat' products i.e. butter, cheese, whole milk, lard … I have effectively become afraid of such foods; they are the enemy. Taking the step to swallow any from the barred list remains such a frightening task though I know, I know, I should.

It's like in cartoons when you have a little angel in a cloud on one side and a little devil in a flame on the other. One force is telling me that I have to get out of this ASAP and that unless I pull myself together and get back into healthy eating habits I will keep on drifting further and further away from myself and to a point of no return. Yet another force is restraining me. And although that little devil has absolutely no argument to reason with my angel, and the angel should in theory be so much more persuasive, somehow the rascal always seems to succeed in winning me over.

I have reached a stage where I am worried to tears when a meal is not prepared precisely the way I would like it to be, or worse still when my plate displays a food I had not planned to eat. The really inexplicable thing is that I actually am hungry, so hungry sometimes, but I have no appetite, and I have such troubles in determining whether what I am eating is enough or not, or normal, or not.

I feel so much more fragile physically, but above all emotionally. It works in a spiral, or like the dog chasing its tail. I am not sure how much the upset mind drags the body down versus the impact my weight-loss consequently has on my way of thought. I feel vulnerable. I have been going out less and less, not to mention rigidly cutting down on alcohol! I am secluding myself even from my closest friends, and possibly losing them too.

But here is where you enter the scene. I feel at home, comfortable, closer to myself than at any other point in the day when I'm you – and Spence and Ali. You give me confidence, faith, hope and assurance. You inspire me with your happy-go-lucky charm; the drive I need to head my way out of this mess. When I am with you it feels like the alter-ego is suffocated and somehow fades away – I feel once more 99 per cent me!

I could have stayed on at college this term, continuing to fool around with that other 1 per cent that is still lost, cheat myself and live only half the life I long to live. I could have continued to pretend, but every beguiling detail is both unfair to you, all of you, and will eventually cost me if not my life, then at least the occasion of perpetuating such existence. And I want so much to be a mother one day.

Phew! I do hope this letter had its desired effect in explaining things as best as I can. And that it isn't all too heavy stuff. Please promise me that this will only serve to better your understanding of where I am coming from, and where I am at, and will in no way change your attitude towards me. I am playing it open because I trust you and you all deserve to know what's going on.

Love,
Swiss-Miss

This letter to Sam was prescient in so many ways. Sam and I were to share the greater part of our lives together in future, but, for now, we were still 'just friends'.

10

Strike two. I thought I had rid myself of the horror for good, yet here I was again. I had slid down the snake's back; all the way down to square one. Then a little further back still.

Because this time it was a little harder. It was a little more twisted and the knots were that much more difficult to untangle. This time there was less joy when I put on a few hundred grams, less of a sense of achievement; no delight at the thought of 'getting better'. It had been a tiring walk up a muddy mound and I had slipped back down to the bottom. Now the hill had turned into a mountain, and the mount felt steeper beneath my feet.

I woke up early every morning, famished, drawn out of bed to the drilling sound of hunger. And as I broke my fast so the day would begin, one long, empty, food chain. And all I could think of was food. It was a daily dialogue inside, drawing schedules and plans all revolving around fixed menus and set mealtimes. It was exhausting. And in darker

hours, I could not sleep. Lying for too long on one side cut
the circulation from under me as there was no padding to
cushion the nerves from my bones. One night I dreamed
that I was walking through a gigantic supermarket, pushing
a trolley gargantuan in size. And the trolley filled with
colourful treats as I paced up one aisle and slowly down the
next. I woke up with that image still vivid, so real, at the
forefront of my mind. But I couldn't remember arriving at
the till. I am not sure whether I ever made it out with brimming paper shopping bags.

There was more cheating this time.

4 March 2002

So Cruella has come back to pay a visit ... I would rather
not think that I have let her in for good, but she seems to
have her way more often than she should. What I hate
above all is that I have recently found myself cheating more
than once. Before, I simply used to put loads of veggies on
my plate and put the cereal or meat underneath so as to
make it look like there is even more hiding beneath the veg.
But now I take the bottle of olive oil and pretend to pour
some out with emphatic swirling gestures over my plate
without ever allowing anything to trickle out. If anyone is

watching, I pour a careful amount on to the side of my plate then barricade it from my meal with a piece of food which I then proceed to scatter over my plate once I have finished what I did intend to eat so as to give the dish an oily shine.

I also serve myself well and then get up for seconds when no one has seen my plate and throw any extra – unwanted – food back into its serving dish. I have found myself throwing out yoghurt pots half full, giving the impression that they were duly emptied or even, on occasion, scrapes of food on my own plate if I can make it to the bin and cover it up with paper towel.

I wake up in the morning earlier than anyone else so that I can choose what I want to eat, without supervision. I often take the butter out of the fridge and leave it sitting visibly on the table so that it appears to have been spread on my toast. But in fact not even the smallest knob goes anywhere near my slice of bread. When we have chicken I take a piece and squeeze it in my napkin when no one is looking my way so as to pump out every last ounce of grease.

The other day we were driving back from Italy and my dad had prepared a picnic for the car. There were veggie sticks for me and two hard-boiled eggs with a couple of rice cakes. Every care of the world had been put towards ensuring this would be a meal I could enjoy and munch at

happily in the sun together with everyone else. I received my
bundle with thanks, and took a stack of napkins too. My
egg yolks were carefully wrapped up in one of the napkins
and thrown into the rubbish bag along with everyone else's
trash. I told my father I had wolfed down my lunch in full.

All this in order to not exceed a calorific count by the
end of the day, one that 'I' consider acceptable.

And yet I am floating in my trousers; I feel too thin at
times; and above all I no longer have my period. If only I
could go back to perfect shape and period without having to
stuff myself to get there.

I hate myself for all these things. Swarmed with guilt
and drowning in remorse. But I remain confident that soon
I will want to read all this again only to confess it all to my
parents and above all to smile at the thought of its all
belonging to a murky past of mine.

I am not smiling as I read through these entries, shocked
rather to think that this is not that distant in the past.
Afraid, even, that it will come back to bite me if I am not
careful. I still feel at risk. I think it would be more alarming
if I didn't. I had forgotten half of these things, selective
memory playing its self-protective role. But I am so
thankful that I have it all written down, never to forget,

always to hear the words written by my very hand though dictated, perhaps, by another voice. It is so important not to let it slip away.

I was staying at my grandmother's house in Headington, ten minutes away from Oxford city centre. It was on one of the fortnightly weekends spent back there when I was due to hand in essays and sit double tutorials. My parents were with me that time and we were all having dinner at home. There was chicken, rice and a garden-full of steamed vegetables on offer. The house knew about my circumstances and always made sure that whatever was on the menu would be tailored in a small separate dish to fit within the tight bounds of my comfort zone. This way, at least, they knew I would eat without restraint and perhaps, even, with measured amounts of pleasure. But my allocated portion of chicken was a size above what I (*She? It? We?*) was willing to accept. Our emptied dishes had already been brought back to the kitchen and everyone had nearly finished their course. It seemed I was left with no other option but to eat mine up too, but I could not summon the courage to jump.

The napkin.

It was a large, creamy-white, trimmed cloth napkin sitting comfortably across my lap. There was a moment of hesitation. But then there was not. They were all in great discussion and I had said enough to avert any suspicious glances darting my way. It was the swift gesture of a thief. And while my heart throbbed with shame, Cruella whispered proud words of praise to my ear.

The napkin folded, the plate empty, we all retired to watch the news.

The following evening we all sat at table for dinner. My parents, my grandmother and I, the bandit without a blush. Food ready to serve, plates neatly stacked, napkins neatly arranged. I unfolded mine to rest on my lap, and it was damp. Now a flush of red blotched at my cheek. Nothing had been said. The napkin had been found, the chicken wrapped inside it too. The chicken had been thrown out, the napkin had been hand-washed, and now it was returned to me damp. A not-so-subtle way of letting me know, from the kitchens, that my scam had been uncovered.

When I was first thrown into the boxing ring I was able to dodge the harder knocks because I still had the double-jointed suppleness of a child. And while I had been crinkled, crumpled and crunched, yet there was still enough give for me to leap back into shape. This time the springs had lost their bounce. I could feel a rigidity turning cold in my bones.

I remember one scene that speaks so much of this stiffness greater than it ever was before. The absurdity of these situations is so telling too; how awry, how distorted, how wrong is this disease. Cruella steals the best of you and inhabits your essence at the core. She makes you say unspeakable things and believe unthinkable thoughts. She is a fraud, a swindler and a cheat. We were going on holiday and needed to be ready by lunch. The plan had been to grab an early bite and leave. That way we avoided motorway food and didn't have to stop for too long on the side of the road. That was okay. I knew that was the plan. But it was 11:30am when my dad called me down to eat. Only two hours after my breakfast and that had not yet been digested through. My stomach was not grumbling now: it still felt crammed with food. Midday was a decent time for lunch; 11:30 was not. That was senseless and stupid and my blood began to boil. And so the headmistress bossed around, furious. And she stomped upstairs to her room and turned around in circles, incensed.

Then it was 12:00 and so I settled down. We had our meal and left in sunshine. But that episode belonged to a series on dizzying repeat.

11

I was in the car with my mum, driving home from a sunny morning of smiles and positive attitude all round. We were in the car on our way back from having been shopping for food after going to a relaxing yoga class together. I was feeling high and hopeful. Mum asked me what I felt like for lunch, finishing her enquiry with a suggestion of her own. I don't remember what I said I *did* feel like eating, but I know there was no protein listed on the order because I can still hear her retort, 'And what about your protein?! ... Dr D said you had to have protein. You cannot carry on like this, we *must* shift into fifth gear. I am complaisant to your disease feeding you these meals. You will not put on weight with this kind of food, you are heading straight for disaster ...' and then a string of fears, all headed with a capital 'You' and ending with an exclamatory sigh. I read her concern as blame and that perceived accusation translated into guilt; sickening guilt. I began to cry; she continued to shout. We arrived home. I ate what she gave me, including the hard-boiled egg. She then presented me with a home-made apple compote, my favourite, that she had lovingly prepared, with no added sugar. But I declined, softly, with fingers crossed that she would see the effort I had already made. Yet my refusal sparked a renewed outburst, propelling me to my room with a slam of the door so loud I can still hear it today, banging against my heart.

I cried so much it hurt. There are a few occasions I can remember when my tears turned into a visceral cry, pulling every emotion out of my gut. When everything around me turned black and the end of the tunnel suddenly became filled with iron-clad cement. The kind of tears that cut the wind out of your breath give you a stomach ache, they work the muscles so hard. The sort of tears that leave you drained and numb when they eventually dry.

I couldn't do the home thing any more. I needed to leave. My house had turned into a sanatorium and my parents had become doctor, nurse, cook, supervisor all at once. Once-healthy bonds of love and care were tainted by clinical concern. Their parental tendencies to protect me and tend to my every need was overwritten by the obligation to treat me with near medical expertise. Boundaries were becoming blurred and when emotions took over it all spun out of control.

My mother walked into my room to find me clinging to

a teddy bear, wiping my nose in his woolly scarf because I had run out of tissues and could not bring myself to go find more. She calmed me down. She said she was sorry. She explained, like so many times before, that there was nothing more painful for a mother than to see her own child literally evaporating before her eyes. That feeling of helplessness when faced with my occasional interjections; the sense of guilt to think that she might in fact be in compliance with my disease, preparing meals that I would eat and padding my comfort zone with cushions of protection that ultimately had me moving nowhere forward – all these things meant that once in a while it was inevitable that she too would snap. Where to draw the line between making sure that I felt safe enough to make confident steps forward but not ceding so much to my fears that I ended up stuck in a rut? How to discern between the genuine weeping of her little girl and the twisted complaints of the mean thing that was haunting her inside? When to get angry and forceful and when, instead, to show compassion laced with soothing reassurance? These were questions that hammered at her all day. Only now can I begin to understand what she had to go through, she and my father.

After she had kissed me and hugged me and drawn out a smile I would never have found on my own, we talked about the possibility of my going away to be cared for in expert hands. My father joined in on the discussion later that evening and although they heard what I was saying and understood my reservations about continuing the way we were going, still they were adamant that I would be miserable in such an institution where I would hate every meal because it would not be the sort of food I ever liked and it would be served only with the aim to plump me up like a goose. There were also reasoned concerns about my being pumped with drugs, turned to a vegetative state that was altogether easier for the staff to handle. We talked and talked and I assured them that I wanted to get better more than anything else. But that I was torn between the child inside asking only to be taken care of and the growing daughter determined to show her parents that she could do it on her own. Then there was the added twist of a third voice behind the other two, the one that ordered my demise. It was so hard, at times, to recognise which was which.

We decided, together, that I would stay at home for the time being and continue to work together, our team, to beat it. That night we had pasta and I was allowed to help myself without comment. The olive oil was given a gentle, silent nudge in my direction and no one looked as I poured a drop into my dish. It all felt okay again. For now.

Yet the scales continued to dilly dally and meanwhile the clock was tick-tocking away. I could not afford to lose another gram, but I was not gaining any weight either.

Soon alarm bells were signalled and echoed with threats I now knew all too well. Once more there were gruelling tears and arduous discussions at home, and I could not help but feel shamefaced, guilt-ridden, unworthy – worthless.

5 March 2002 (aged 18)

I am so so so so so so so drained and worn out.

I thought I had it in me to do this alone, but it is now beyond my grasp as every day, hour, minute, I feel myself gradually fading and see me from an ever-growing distance.

Today was the last chance I had to show that I would gain weight out of hospital; I have not put on an ounce. So I am now, in theory, due to be hospitalised. I have just spent the whole day fighting, discussing, reasoning and arguing the pros and cons with my parents, doctors – and indeed myself (my who?). After much cogitation, agitation and lamentation I think we have managed to come up with some kind of a working solution. I will no longer be allowed to set foot in the kitchen – let alone go shopping for food – and every meal will come served on a plate: no discussion.

Like this, we will really be replicating the hospital

scenario, much more than we have done till now, only I will have the 'consolation' of knowing still that even if it is no longer 'food of predilection' (then again, what actually is left that I would really accept nowadays?) that I am being fed, at least it will be good quality (even tasty, with time) food, cooked only with love and genuine care.

My father will find out the exact amount of calorie intake that I should be administered daily, as I would in a clinic, and will devise a concrete timetable to be followed. I will still have a small amount of freedom during the day, when at school and for snacks, but everything I eat will go on a chart that I have drawn on a Word document and I like to call my 'Recovery Action Plan' where you have one field for foods, one field for quantities (both of which I am to fill) and then fields for lipid, carbohydrate and protein contents as well as one for calorie.

This will involve a lot of tears, lassitude, and sometimes despair, but at the end of the day if I don't take the bull by its horns right now, then seconds turn into minutes and into hours, days, months, years – a lifetime (or lack thereof) wasted in waiting?

I just don't have the strength in me this time to fight the devil anymore. Because for every choice one usually takes without even thinking, I take so much time. And every moment of tortuous calculation (should I eat one more spoonful? Should I accept an extra slice? Can I afford to

add a drop of oil on the grand scale of exercise spent
today?...) costs me such a headache that I then feel too tired
to turn any eventual decision into action. So now someone
else will do the thinking for me and even if it means I lose
control of the situation – which is the very core and pit of
this hole in which I linger – it means I will have to learn
to trust myself (the real me) enough to be able to trust
others.

But that is so hard.

I remember arriving back at Oxford for my first double tutorial and to hand in the essays I had written. Everyone so warm and welcoming. Smiles and hugs and eggshells all around. We were all going to go out for dinner. Dinner; restaurant; menu unknown, no chance to talk to the waiters beforehand; and I hadn't eaten in the plane; and I was cold and hungry and I needed to eat something. The general consensus was to take me to the Indian down the road. Having never been to a curry house before, my impression of Indian food was one of plain boiled rice with a pinch of spice and perhaps a side order of sliced cucumber. It was bound to be my safest bet on the grand scale of student life out. I ordered a vegetable curry, bliss-fully unaware that my vegetables would not be steaming with the fresh clean scent of nothing-added. My plate arrived, the food was swimming in viscous, greasy goo. It was brown, with brownish shades of green, and the occasional white speck where rice had not yet absorbed the muck. I gulped. I swallowed. I began to shake and could feel my face flushed with worry, holding back the tears, desperate for an escape. But no one else could see a thing; they didn't know and I didn't want to tell. I could hear them chat away, I could hear the sound of my chewing, I could hear the numbers dancing through my head; calories counted in a desperate struggle for reassurance. And through and through I could hear Cruella sneer, snigger and scold.

8 March 2002

If only I could purge my body of the foul, dirty, unhealthy food I just swallowed tonight … I went to an Indian and had rice with vegetables in a very greasy spice sauce and I simply cannot deal … I feel sick; I am freezing cold but would like to open all the windows and burn off the filth I swallowed … I can no longer think. Too tired …

There are other episodes that I cannot shift from my memory. Images that prance around as real as the day they occurred. One in particular marks the time I spent in Geneva that term. And it illustrates the punitive way in which I was treated over there.

I had a 4 p.m. appointment with Dr D. This fell right when I would normally sit down for my afternoon teatime. And that snack couldn't be pushed forward because that was too close to lunch, which meant that my stomach wouldn't be ready. And if it was pushed back to after seeing the doctor that would then be too close to dinner which meant that my stomach would still feel full by the time I was called to table. So I went without having had anything to eat – and secretly hopeful that it might go unnoticed. The first thing she asked me was what I had had for tea. And I went blank. I couldn't bring myself to lie but I also knew where she was heading and a lump came to sit in my throat as my chest began to thump. 'Come on Emily, you aren't going to let her win are you? You are stronger than that. Come on, let's go downstairs to the cafeteria; they have a selection of things you might like. My treat.' I went because she had tapped into my self-esteem. As calculations hopped and skipped around in my head, they formed equations of ways in which I might be able to make it all okay.

We stepped into the cold neon lights of the hospital cafeteria. She, head of the Eating Disorders Unit, with me walking one step behind, obviously not a friend joining her on a break. And glares pinched me in the back as we made our way to the counter. There was no fruit. Not on that counter. There were cakes and tarts: apple, plum, chocolate, lemon. I chose apple. Its ratio of fruit to jelly-pastry-cream was the most favourable of the lot. But she chose the lemon tart for me; and so, with my meek objections gone unheard, the lemon tart it would be. We moved on to pay and order drinks. I chose tea. But she nodded in disapproval. I chose orange juice. But she chose hot chocolate for me. The man at the counter looked at me, then looked at her; then turned the switch for steaming whole fat milk to fill a mug, and placed a sachet of chocolate powder on the saucer, with two sugars upon her request.

We made our way to a table, in the middle of the room, where stares could shoot from all directions. The lemon tart sat before me a fluorescent yellow competing with the neon lights above; a slice of candied lemon placed neatly on top in a lame effort to display some evidence of the fruit. The chocolate powder streamed into the milk as she shook the sachet to ensure its content was fully emptied. Then the two sugars plunged in next and then a vigorous mixing with the spoon so there could be no sediment sneaking its way to the bottom of the mug where it might be left untouched. And there she sat with her coffee (black, one sugar), and waited; I felt numb all over and though it was my hand cutting spoonfuls of the tart and though it was my arm bringing food and drink to my mouth, yet I was no longer conscious of those movements and I swallowed through choking tears. It was something out of the Big Screen.

I arrived home a zombie. My parents were furious. Everyone agreed that was a step too far. Everyone declared that even they, in their right minds, would not have chosen to give me such a large and heavy combination of food. But what nobody understood was that I was in desperate need of reassurance, not sympathy. Their outrage and commiseration served only to underline the fact that I had, indeed, eaten way too much and that it had in fact been a real indulgence and so, it followed, I should without a doubt be mortified.

And perhaps what frightened me most of all was that it had tasted good. It was, again, the same fear of giving into something that had grown so huge with time: temptation. The dread of its magnitude and of the irreparable damage that could be caused by my surrendering myself to its lure. And in my religion of abstinence, *temptation* was considered the sin of all sins.

Nonetheless, just as before, I did begin to regain weight – and strength. Just as before, the more I stretched the more flexible I became again. The more I gradually let go of control, the more willing I was to let go still further. Every day I scribbled away on my 'Recovery Action Plan' with utter honesty all the things that I had had to eat.

Every evening my father added up with his little manual of calories in one hand and calculator in the other. And whenever I was lagging underneath the set total intake as defined by Dr D, my dad and I would agree, together, to the extra bits and pieces I could nibble before going to bed as an extra push to get me playing by the rules – three honey wholegrain organic biscuits and a banana would be a good idea; two squares of fructose-sweetened 70 per cent dark chocolate and a berry-flavoured soya yoghurt would do the trick. I could choose from a predetermined list. Secretly, I took naughty pleasure in these fixed late-night top-ups. They were like the raspberry-flavoured cough syrup that causes children to make up a cold! I was being prescribed a treat – and that was the only way I could treat myself for a while. Then, on the occasions that I had 'done well' I would beg to know, in as subtle a way as I could conceive, what *exactly* he meant by 'well' (were we talking just literally what I needed to pass my daily calorific count? had I drastically exceeded the guidelines?? was I toppling into no-go-scary-red-zone?) Dad would just smile – and ask Cruella to take a jump. Which, eventually, she did.

By the beginning of spring, and the time of starting my third term, my rosy cheeks were back, my (slight) curves had returned and we felt that I was altogether back in shape. And from my positive point of view I chose not to look ahead in search of possible mountains to come. At home we decided it was okay – and constructive – for me to go back to Oxford and join my friends for what was always considered the most beautiful term of the three, when everyone was outside, parties were thrown and the atmosphere was altogether one of giggles and joy. My parents thought it was important for me to enjoy myself and pursue as normal a life as I now could once more. I agreed. They, and I, believed that being a part of it all, surrounded by people my age and allowing myself to savour the taste of fun, could in fact do me so much more good, in so many other ways, than the rigour of hospital runs and daily clinical care. All this provided I was both physically and mentally in a capacity to enjoy it too. We agreed that I was; Dr D was adamantly against this. By this stage I was back on antidepressants but I also wanted to stop. She was all the more unyielding. She made it clear that if I was to return it would be without her medical consent and that, as such, she could no longer carry on seeing me as a patient. Heads bashed against one another for a while, but eventually there was a general consensus reached that maybe Dr D's methods were not suited for me.

And so I returned to Oxford with a smile. It was the happiest of terms, possibly the best I ever had. I look back and remain convinced that it was right for me to go back from all points of view – save that of Dr D – and for all the reasons outlined above. I was surrounded by my friends, who were aware of the situation from the start, and with whom I had continued to be frank throughout. And although they could not even begin fully to understand where I was coming from, still they were so patient, supportive and accepting. I learned again to laugh. My laughter was setting me free.

I sat my first-year exams with everyone else and celebrated with everyone else on the last day of class. The sense of accomplishment that came from pursuing what I had set out to realise was enormous. It rubbed off my tarnished self-esteem and gave it a promising shine. With medical supervision, I did bring my antidepressant treatment to an end. I enjoyed the sunshine and my heart felt light as a bird let go of its cage. I was awarded a distinction and a further diploma of honour for my academic achievements throughout the year. But my real trophy was the simple smile I carried around with me every day. Friendship is the most meaningful therapy of all.

That summer we went on a road trip: five best friends from university, two cars, house-hopping through France and across to Italy before finishing in Geneva. When I try to immerse myself in feelings of utter happiness I hark back to that journey. It was pure freedom. I sometimes wish there were a magic formula or a chant I could hum before going to sleep and wake up feeling the way I did then.

But imagination is a powerful tool and sometimes just by

visualising that space of mind it can be created to such a degree of truth that I can escape there for a little while, long enough to recover inner calm. It is a very valuable device.

On that holiday I did eat with everyone else, but I did not eat exactly what everyone else was eating. They would have chicken thighs marinated in oily spices; I would have chicken breast marinated in spicy lemon juice. They would snack on crisps and chocolate bars at midnight; I would munch my way through a (large) pack of wholegrain crunchy cereal and 0 per cent Actimel. They all delighted in a seven-course dinner at a fancy restaurant one evening; I had something to eat beforehand and joined in with a diet Coke. Did that mean that I was 'unwell'? I was eating – and enjoying – real quantities of food; I was gladly sharing my meals with the group and sitting at the table without feeling uneasy or self-conscious. I was not able to let go and follow suit with junk food or anything too greasy (um, with any oil at all). But then again do we really have to eat absolutely everything anyone ever serves up on our plate? Wasn't it okay for me to know where my limits lay and to work my way around them so that I could take pleasure in being with my friends; relaxed, relieved, happy? The rest would come with time, naturally. I wouldn't force it and it would just slip back into my habits without my even noticing, just like many other things had done. Was I deluding myself? Was Cruella deluding me? Where do you draw the line between focusing still on what little there is left 'wrong' to fix or concentrating rather on the good things so that they become more and more real to the point of crushing out the bad?

So it is that I entered year two, beaming. The wound felt healed again. This time 'for real' – no more circular recovery schemes; I was now 'well', well and truly. On 11 November 2002 Sam Taylor became my boyfriend. He had been on the road trip too; we were best of friends before anything else. I felt loved, wanted, perhaps even pretty at times. It was all happiness, giggles and holding hands down the street. Little did I know how supportive he would almost immediately become.

Soon after, even my period returned and I was made 'woman' once more. As before, I was only too thrilled when I found my pants spotted with red. As before, I ran out the toilet and dashed this time into Sam's room where all my closest friends were having tea. I announced the thing as though I had just given birth. To which they, who had been so supportive from the moment I had opened up, all cheered. And we laughed at how bizarre a scene it was for any outsider to observe.

Nearly a year on from the Christmas I was told to stay back home, and a second loop had been drawn to a close. Everything, once again, had returned to 'normal'.

12

It was 1 March 2003, term two of my second year at Oxford. I remember walking back to college that evening – but I do not remember where I had been. It was still cold towards the middle of term two and we were all wrapped up. I remember trotting merrily along the quad with Sam by my side. Other friends were with us too – but their faces are blurred. I know I was happy because the stab that followed felt all the more sharp. The phone rang. I was told that Isabelle, my first 'best friend', my childhood friend, the friend you do not feel the need to keep in touch with every day because it is a given that yours is a closeness too strongly rooted to be blown away, had been killed in a car accident. Gone. At first I hid behind a shield of mistrust, throwing the news on to a pile of rumours typical to small cities with nothing much to do. I was shocked to hear that two girls had been killed in a car crash, but the horror was no more than a suspension of disbelief as experienced from the comfort of a cinema chair with a tub of popcorn in one hand.

I walked to my room and decided to call a mutual friend of Isabelle's and mine, simply for peace of mind. I remember her voice trembling as she confirmed the news. I was standing against the wall in the long corridor that led to my room; I felt myself sink to the ground. My brain went numb; my hands were cold. It was not pain that I felt; I could not feel a thing. After a while – I am not sure how long – I managed to pull myself up to a puppet-like standing stance and walked to the kitchen to tell Sam. I heard someone say: 'She was my oldest friend but I hadn't seen her for a while … we took it for granted that our paths would always continue to cross … There were four of them in the car … a motorbike came in the other direction … tried to avoid him … went flying into the fields … too late … gone.' I saw the look of alarm on their faces and I heard the same voice say she needed to lie down.

In my room, in the dark, my eyes began to sting and the warm tears trickled down to land on shoulders that could not bear the weight. The door opened with an offensive beam of light. Sam walked towards me in silence and held me tight like a rag doll that has been picked up off a pavement in the rain. I began to feel the pain of her death, but it was that overwhelming sense of guilt that I continue to feel most vividly of all. I felt guilty because we hadn't spoken for a few years; I had been annoyed with her for mixing with a group of which I did not approve; I felt guilty because how could I therefore deserve to grieve her loss? Was I one of 'those'? Those who spring to such morbid occasions as the perfect excuse to turn the spotlight on to themselves; who rename themselves 'best friend' or 'greatest admirer' of the deceased to shed crocodile tears before a sympathetic crowd. How selfish. How self-absorbed. And the numbness was branching out of my brain, invading my veins like a poison, dripping through my every limb.

I called my parents and my father answered the phone. As usual, wasting no pennies on a quick hello, I asked him to call me back. But the voice that spoke to him sent shivers down his spine and his immediate reaction was one of anger. Convinced that my broken chords were due to an emotional teenage break-up with Sam, his customary 'For God's sake, child' outburst was one he soon came sorely to regret. I know my father and when I use the word anger it is for lack of a better term. When his pitch is most cold and his tone sounds most cross it is generally because he is faced with a situation where he sees those he loves hurt in a way he cannot repair. My mother called me back and I heard myself utter the same string of words: 'Isabelle … car crash … Spain … dead.' It felt calming to hear her sanction my sorrow and shun my shame for feeling the way I did. It felt comforting to hear that I *had* to come back for the funeral, that I *should* call Laurent, Isabelle's (twin) brother, because he would be needing support from those who knew him well and that I *must* write to her parents too.

I woke up the following morning convinced for a fleeting moment that it had all been a dreadful nightmare; none of it was real. But my all-too-puffy eyes gave the lie to that. Sam asked me to go with him to hand an in essay due that morning. It was a ten-minute stroll and the fresh air would do me good. I ambled along as if on a travelling carpet – walking without legs, utterly detached from the movements my body was performing. We stopped off at a coffee shop on the way back. It was crowded but the faces were hazy and distorted; it was noisy but the sound was muffled and warped. I wanted to be back in my room, in the dark, alone.

I spoke to Laurent later that day, fearful as I dialled his number that he would not want to talk to me, see me, know me. But he was so pleased that I had called and he seemed to want for me to be around. I returned to Geneva having not changed for three days; my hair still tied up in a knot. Isabelle's house was an open-door invitation for all friends and family to join before the funeral. I entered with a large group and felt a speck amongst the mass. They all went to kiss her mother first, and she greeted them with what little strength she had. At last I tentatively made my way towards her. She looked at me, held me in her arms and whispered softly in my ear: 'Thank you for helping me to cry.' Briefly, I let go of the reins I had tightly secured around any feeling of compassion and kindness towards myself. Momentarily it was okay for me to be sad. But already a twisted spirit was looming; the shadows of the room were seeping through my skin as my past came creeping along with it, crawling inside of me, pushing me out of the way.

I had to see her. I had to because to me the concept of death belonged to wide screens and grandfathers. I had to because I needed to talk to her, in silence. Because I wanted to be in a room with her just one last time; close my eyes and pretend we were little girls. My mother came with me. We punched in the code to enter. We walked into a salmon-pink reception area with a few odd-fitting chairs scattered about in a vain attempt to make the room welcoming. On either side were doors painted a darker shade of the same nauseating pink, and numbered. I thought I would always remember the number to her cell, but I don't. My mother came in with me, into a small square room; lilies everywhere and candles of her favourite scent. A man, whom I later recognised to be a mutual friend's father, was standing by her coffin, tranquil. I waited a few steps behind him, hoping he would be sensitive enough to feel that his was now one presence too many. He did. I moved forward. She was dressed in a white muslin nightdress; the coffin only disclosed the upper half of her body and she seemed smaller than the graceful gazelle I knew her to be. Her face was layered with foundation and then waxed. My mother looked at me and asked with a whisper whether I wanted to be alone. I nodded. My heart stopped. The door quietly clicked shut. I took the time to think all the thoughts I wanted to transmit; perhaps I said a few out loud – I cannot remember exactly what I said. I tried to tell of my longing for her to return; for us to get our two paths back on to the same track; to know that she would light a spark inside of me to say that she was near. I walked out, out of her booth and out from the odd-looking chairs, and crossed the corridor where my mother was speaking to the man. He kindly said hello, but I buried my face against my mother's chest and began to weep. The scene I had just witnessed came straight out of a twisted horror film; it was not the peace-making experience I had wanted. She was not there; just a body decked in white, with a strange-looking mask, and the smell of lilies oozing through my pores. I had felt her presence more in all the minutes preceding that moment – and all the hours that followed. She was not in that room, and so she must be elsewhere: this gave me faith. And yet I had to see her. I had to, perhaps, because a part of me was already seeking comfort in torment.

From the moment that phone first rang I began once more to hold back on food. Food, to me, was associated with merit and reward. To eat was to lack respect for my friend who had died. To eat was to deny the violence of the situation. To hear myself munch away at food was vulgar and wrong. Looking back, I was trying desperately to hold on to my last scrap of control over existence. In a time when big questions were sizzling in my mind the only way for me to keep on top of myself was to hold back on the very fuel that I could decide would allow me to live.

It took a long time for me to shake myself out of an anaesthetised state. Then one early morning I woke up with the words dancing through my head. Finally I was finding a way to express the aching that stifled my heart. Finally I was beginning to connect with the weeping girl inside …

May 2003 (aged 19)

Stolen future from a golden past
But the present of her presence in our hearts for ever cast.

A sparkle in her eyes become a twinkle little star
Sending comfort from the skies, so close yet still too far.

The story of a child become an angel under the moon,
The journey of a dove's flight up above a life gone too soon.

The portrait of a friendship painted with a rhyme,
The poem of a beauty framed by the hands of time.

I hear the giggle of a girl, I hear her sing a song.
I hear happiness, I hear joy, I hear the smile for which I long.

I read the diaries of a princess, I dream of Christmas in my
  sleep.
I read the chapter of our childhood; memories o'er I shall
  not weep.

Anger turns to pain and the unspoken regret
Of all that could have been if she hadn't left us yet.

If only I could tell her; if we hadn't wasted days
Assuming our distance was but a teenage trivial phase.

I want to turn the pages, I want to come to when
After worn out ages we finally meet again.

I want my pen to scribble, words to comprehend
Why 'once upon a time' sprinted for 'the end'.

But bitter tears for lost souvenirs serve only to puzzle the
  mind
And drown our soul with the sour taste of true love left
  behind.

So let the pain subside, let the hurting abate
Accept the awful truth; accept the twist of fate.

And as the clouds begin to lift, lily-flowers drift; a rainbow
*   will appear,*
Then my soul begins to beat as I sense the feel so sweet of
*   her magic coming near.*

Worries gone astray, I put my feelings to the test;
Hopeful I kneel to pray and put my distress to the rest.

I close my eyes and realise the time has come: let go
She resides right by my side; she knows I miss her so.

She whispers in the night: I needn't be in fright; she
*   promises to stay*
She whispers softly in my ear: I mustn't live in fear; things
*   will be okay.*

She wants me to laugh, she wants me to live; she asks me to
*   forgive my sorrow*
So I will laugh and I will live and I will dance like there's
*   no tomorrow.*

I felt rested once I laid this poem on paper. There was a lightness I had not felt for a while. Perhaps that morning spelled more than just a poem; perhaps it was a 'defining moment', a 'turning point' on the greater scale of my life so far – but the balance still fell in favour of a heavier weight. I still had a long journey set ahead of me before I would be freed of a heart laden with lead. Cruella still was clenching hard on my soul and I had yet to find the tools to deliverance.

13

The summer leading to my final year I gradually felt myself slip from over the cloud, and the white fluffy cloud turned darker shades of grey as the days moved on.

I didn't see it happen and I never really noticed any clear-cut change; perhaps because far beneath the polished surface not all that much was different.

It was the way I behaved with Sam that soon became the benchmark for how rapidly things were – *I* was – deteriorating. At first our hands were laced, then we would simply walk side by side, and then he held my hand like that of a child. But that summer I pushed him away. I didn't want to be touched; any loving stroke felt like an invasion. Sometimes, when I was tired, or anxious, and felt even more vulnerable than usual, I would crawl into my skin with the sense of imaginary fat deposits on my thighs. I literally believed that they were swelling by the second. My distortions then shot out to target Sam; I would suddenly 'notice' his cheeks double in size from one minute to the next. And the more I felt disgusting, the more I projected disgust on to him. They only ever lasted briefly, these moments, and then I would snap out of myself, apologise in tears, try to explain what was going on. But I was mean, snappy, selfish. Anything around me mirrored the likeness of myself and therefore bore the brunt of my self-hatred. So self-absorbed; there is no room for anyone other than the disease in anorexia. I heard the things I said and regretted them even before I spoke, and yet I still said some horrible things. With him, with everyone, every outburst and all my despicable manners were followed up each time with a note, begging for forgiveness and seeking somehow to explain. I have always been better at expressing my thoughts through the written word. My hand responds to my heart even when my mind is playing wicked tricks on me. In the peace of writing I manage to recollect my thoughts, and find myself again.

Sam and I nearly broke up. I suggested he see someone else; that I wasn't worth the wait; that he had to live the life of a twenty-one-year-old with light-hearted girls who still knew how to laugh, because I no longer had the strength. I even put forward the possibility of his strolling down the streets of Soho so that at least his natural thirst for physical affection could be quenched. But he never once gave up on me. It was this faith, his, that of my family and of select close friends, that kept me together. As they all held firmly to those pieces of me that seemed to be stripping away, so I eventually managed to stitch them back together and move forward. But for now I was still a worn-out rag doll.

That summer I decided to go and see a hypnotherapist. Someone needed to help draw my disorder out of me. It was too deeply rooted: it had welded itself in parts of me I didn't even know. I felt I would only be able to untangle that knot by shutting my eyes and coming face to face with my demon inside. I had no idea what to expect, but I knew it had worked for some. My uncles had quit smoking from one day to the next through hypnotism. Perhaps, then, such methods could also help me quit hating myself, hurting myself, harming myself?

I had seen a woman give a talk at Oxford and remembered how impressed I was when she had managed to teach the audience, within a couple of minutes, how to put our hand to sleep through the mere power of 'thought'. I was hoping she could now do the same with the hand that was at my throat. It was a hot sunny day and I crossed through the park with a bag full of hope swinging by my side. Sam would meet me an hour later in the waiting room. I could already imagine his face lighten up when he saw in my eyes that the darkness had disappeared.

She came to meet me, the woman I had seen onstage. And I was immediately struck by a spooky sensation. There was something ghostly about her and unsettling about her ways. She led me downstairs to her office where I was welcomed by a black shiny armchair with ample space to unwind. She started to talk me through the process, with a voice that sounded phony, and asked me whether I had any questions before we began. I was tempted to ask to leave. Instead I agreed to begin. Then the womb of leather magically tipped me into a horizontal stretch and I was told, in a whisper, to close my eyes. There was no honey in her voice, nothing soothing, nothing sweet. Instead, her words were embalmed in artificial saccharine syrup that was gradually causing me to feel woozy. I was told to imagine a little girl, the one I had spoken about before the light had been switched off. I was told to take that little girl by the hand and walk with her down a long stairwell down to the abyss. I was told to carry on walking down, down these stairs, towards unknown shadows. And to walk faster and faster down, breaking now into a run, faster down those stairs, holding that little girl's hand and not to fear. Not to fear because everything was going to be okay and I should just trust myself going down, down those stairs, always further down. And now I should run back up again, run, run back up the stairs. Up the stairs and away from frightening things. Away from frightening things we run up the stairs. A-n-d-10-9-8-7-6-5-4-3-2-1————wake-up.

Back on with the lights; away with treacle undertones. I was advised, strongly, not to discuss my experience with anyone for a while, just to let it sink in. Out with the diary and on to her fees. It would be best if I could pay her in cash, really.

When I met Sam after the session, his expression was hesitant and his eyes were unconvinced. They did not mirror any brightness from my own. I had been; I had paid; I had left nothing behind. I stepped outside glazed with anguish, and it stuck to me for days.

I am *not* saying that hypnotherapy is a scam. I *am* saying that it is not a game. I cannot tell whether I actually ever was hypnotised because I never tried it again. I can declare that whatever it was did me no good. It is important for me to underline how essential it is for the hypnotist to be found through good references and to be able to prove their qualifications. Perhaps I should have carried on and seen it through with a couple sessions more. But for the time being I preferred to keep my head above ground. No more downward spiral for me. Yet it was clear that I needed assistance in climbing out of the hole into which it seemed I had slipped once again.

I wouldn't go back to see Dr D. Hers was an unnecessarily forceful and aggressive approach which focused entirely on my putting on weight, with the help of little white pills administered with water, and involved an astonishing combination of threats, criticism and reproach. So far her methods had reached no conclusive results. With her, I had twice put on weight and twice seen my period return. All physical suggestions of my disease were treated with utmost urgency every time. But never did we address the underlying issues that caused the sickness to grow and never was I equipped with tools to defend myself against an eventual future strike. As the summer came to a close I was willing to accept that I couldn't simply return to university, completing a four-year course in three, without some kind of a support mechanism set in place.

Patrick and I had what seemed to have become an annual conversation about what I should – could – do to put together an action plan. We spoke about the importance of having someone there to offer psychological relief. Someone neutral I could talk to who would bear no judgement while offering professional feedback. Patrick suggested, this time, that instead of seeing a psychiatrist, who would inevitably steer her sessions from a medical perspective, prescribing drugs and treating symptoms with a clinically scientific approach, I should try to find a psychotherapist. What I needed was more of an individualistic approach where I could be taken care of as a human being in momentary crisis rather than treated as a sickened patient. Once again, Patrick had understood exactly what it was I needed and was able to express it in a way that did not scare me, from the stance of me willing to give it a go, though we both inevitably shed tears in talking.

And so it was, in term one of my third and last year at Oxford, that I met with Louise. She calls herself a *humanistic therapist* and talks to you without looking down at you. Through Louise, I was referred to Vicki who became my nutritionist and helped me to handle surface matters while Louise and I looked into what lay beneath. They both agreed to see me through as far as they could go so long as they felt that I was walking with them in the same direction towards recovery. I later discovered that the two were deeply apprehensive about the risk they were taking in letting me carry on through university and with the prospect of finals looming when physically I could barely walk up a flight of stairs without pausing at every other step to gasp for breath. But they understood the importance of trusting me and helping me regain a sense of self-worth that would then trigger everything else to get back into place like fallen dominoes returning to standing. I would travel to London twice a week to see both nutritionist and therapist, and we were to hold frequent phone consultations in between. That was the plan and it felt reassuring to have one in place.

The first time I went to see Louise it was with hopeful trepidation. I expected clinical antiseptic rooms and stiff yellow plastic chairs; instead there were welcoming armchairs, a water fountain and colourful magazines on display. I anticipated sinister smells; instead there was a sweet comforting aroma oozing from scented candles that cast a glow which gave the rooms a homely feel but not so many as to turn the whole setting into a mystical sham. Neither sterile nor suffocating, it felt just right.

I imagined Louise to be frosty and formal: instead she emanated warmth. I was only familiar with reprimand, threats and censure. Here I heard soft words of reassurance, encouragement and support. Neither too soft nor tyrannically strict; with her I felt just right. And as I stepped out of her offices I was no longer marching to the cautionary drill of fear. This time I was skipping to kind echoes of positive promise.

I learned a new jingle for life that day, one where everything rhymes with 'it's *okay*'.

With Louise I drew links connected directly to core feelings I had grown to disregard. Every recollection I described was pulled straight back to the elementary emotions that were provoked and stripped of any intellectual frills. It was so much more painful to talk in the simple words of a child; and yet – or because – it struck at such deeper chords. It was so much harder to dig beneath the surface of facts and discover the root feelings of whatever story I told. It wasn't about what happened, nor even why;

Perfect

it was all about how whatever happened affected me in most basic terms and seeing ways in which such visceral reactions had become engrained and turned into recurrent behavioural patterns later on.

It is strange how people react, the way I reacted, when confronted with the question: 'How did that make you *feel*?'

First I wiggled about in my now not-so-comfortable seat, like a worm being poked out of a lazy snooze. This was followed by a noise like 'uuummm' with the hope that that might prove a satisfactory reply. Then it became clear that I was expected to deliver more, and so there streamed out an outpouring of vacuous words, richly decorated with intellectual frills, everything academic, nothing really true. And this was rounded out with a laugh, one final attempt at lifting the pressure through comical relief, in vain. All met with silence.

'How are you feeling now?'

At which, inevitably, the abscess does burst. And naked emotions come riding out on a wave of tears.

How difficult it is to recount personal narratives without the all-too-necessary preamble of excuse and a few lines of justification to close. It was about finding the confidence in me not to worry about how my words might be received. Pulling myself away from the permanent trial running in my head and needing no one else to condone – nor condemn – whatever action, thought or impression of mine.

Happy Hurt Guilt Hopeful Relieved Anger Shame Peaceful Sad Lonely Fear Proud Loved Grateful.

I was beginning to learn a new language of emotion. All other terms were derived from here. I had an accent of my own, we all do, but fundamentally they were linguistic skills that I could carry with me anywhere, through life, and always be understood. It was all returning to basics, building real things with my own two hands.

The next step would be for me to learn to melt the mould that had fixed these manners of conduct. I would need to reprogramme the mental pathways that currently led me to feel sad, afraid, undeserving, and ashamed. I would require practical tools to tap into, question, challenge and ultimately reverse certain belief systems engrained that prevented me from flourishing into a natural, happy me. But for the moment the best I could do was to acknowledge where I was at and sit with my itchy feelings till the irritation passed. And, ultimately, it would pass.

Louise taught me to take care of myself. She allowed me to see that the best part of growing up is acknowledging a part of us that always remains a child, and to cherish that child always. I discovered feelings I had not admitted, nor even recognised, in the past. Fear. I was so afraid. Afraid of uncertainty. Afraid of not being good enough. Afraid of disappointing my parents, other people. Afraid that I was not, could not be, perfect.

Louise listened, softly, and she let me ride my feelings like I never had before. With her I also learned about boundaries. I learned about protecting myself from situations that led to my feeling vulnerable. It was about removing myself from such a circumstance without offending anyone else in the process; looking after myself but not to the detriment of others. She taught me to express how I felt in such a way that could only ever be constructive. There can be a devastating breakdown when you present matters from your own point of view, making clear that you are not blaming, not accusing anybody but only that you need to say how certain behaviours or states of affairs make you feel. In my relationship with my parents, with Sam – and with everyone else too – I became more able to voice gut reactions, both pleasant and not.

Instead of collapsing into tears and slamming doors to hide away from any painful place, I now could say, 'When you do *this*, it makes me feel *this way* and, while I cannot ask *you* to change, I can change *my* way of dealing with this, and the first step is to let you know how I am *feeling* right now.'

It sounds almost too simple. And yet, it is astonishing how emotionally retarded we all are and how rare it is that people are able to express themselves this way, drawing their own boundaries and making them clear; understanding the difference between communicating an impression and imposing an opinion. For me, it was mostly about knowing how to say things without being afraid of letting people down, without worrying about how my words would be received and whether I was going to upset anyone by saying what I needed to say. And when I say 'people', or 'anyone', by that I mean above all my parents, my sister, my brother. I do not know why I want so badly to be the *perfect* daughter, the *perfect* sister – and *perfect* therefore in every other way too. I cannot figure out where it comes from, that need to be better than my best and place the level of expectation at an insurmountable height.

Louise taught me to accept, embrace even, my vulnerability, not as a weakness but rather a strength that could allow me to reach out to others in ways not that many people could. I was taught to accept that I cannot control everything in my life, nor everyone around me and that I needed to trust that things would fall into place if I believed in myself – and others. I learned that obsessing about a problem or a worry inevitably leads you straight into that concern, head first. Just like driving a car, it's all about looking directly ahead, keeping a steady hand on the steering wheel, and not staring at any obstacles you are trying to avoid, otherwise you *will* crash.

I was introduced to a little girl. She was standing, lonely, in a corner of my heart. She asked, timidly, if I would look after her, stroke her hair, make her feel loved. I recognised her from photos of me when I was small. It was just a solid shoulder I offered at first. Then my hand tentatively reached out. Years on and I have yet to open my heart to her every day with beaming warmth. But at least, since then, I never walked out on her again. Growing up means embracing who you were while becoming who you are – and loving all of you, without question.

With Louise I began to let go of perfection and learn to love the real me, not the one I was trying to be for everybody else. I am still learning today.

14

Louise made it clear that she did not deal with food, which was why she introduced me to Vicki, whom she knew well. Vicki would look after my diet, make sure not only that I was eating sufficient amounts but above all that I was receiving adequate levels of essential nutrients. Louise believed it was important to address the symptoms of my ailment separately to its cause. I was not used to this approach: until now both aspects had always been jumbled together, with the former taking far greater precedence over the latter.

I had been to see a dietician once before, in Geneva. She was an utter imbecile and the only vivid memory I keep of any time spent in her office is one of fainting by the receptionist's desk after struggling to give several vials of blood. I have fainted twice in my life, both times after a blood test, when my sugar levels plummet to such a low point a natural defence mechanism shuts my body down and takes over until my system can reboot itself. It is a horrible sensation, frightening and totally disorientating. I woke up, both times, feeling every inch a very little girl.

Vicki would feed my brain and my body while Louise worked on delivering my heart and fuelling it with the power of letting go. I believe it was this newfound double approach that was key in opening the door to a stable, long-lasting, recovery. For once, I was able to talk about what was going on inside without mixing it up with the physical manifestation of whatever sadness might have caused. For once, I could talk about my eating without the catch that my calorific accounts would be measured against how I then claimed to feel and that anything I said was pinned upon the backdrop of where I stood on the great big pyramid of food.

Vicki believed in seaweed, tofu, brown rice, wholegrain bread and seeds. She knew about holistic nutrition as well as having a sound, scientific understanding of how the body works and what it requires to function optimally. Here I had found someone who met both ends of my roots – the paternal scientific and the maternal holistic approach – and could listen to my nutritional reports without prejudice. She was not judgemental, that was new too, and there was no hint of criticism in her ways. She was bold enough to trust me and so I, in turn, and with time, became brave enough to trust myself, that 'me' inside whose language I had lost the capacity to understand. I was beginning to hook up with my gut again.

Perfect

Vicki did not dictate weekly meal plans nor send me away with a list of obligatory foods. Vicki did not 'do' dictating. She did not censor; she did not restrict. She was more sensitive than that, and ultimately hers was by far the cleverest approach. I told her what I liked to eat, nothing too dangerous, and what I might be willing to try – in homeopathic dosage. I said I liked vegetables; she (gently) required a minimum variety of three to four per meal. I said I enjoyed couscous, brown rice and other such cooked wholegrains. She kindly asked me to add an extra spoonful every time. Small steps, but moving in the right direction.

Vicki saw where I was standing and knew how far I could pace in one go. She stretched an ample safety net below me and walked by my side. I was not blindfolded this time. We were together on this path. There was no stick served with my carrots. Vicki never made me feel ashamed and never took an angry tone. Hers was not punishment food. It did not leave an acrid medicinal after-taste in the mouth. Her bubbling enthusiasm for texture, flavour, colour and smell was contagious.

I was, as a result, wholly honest with her and just as she trusted me so I began to trust my food. And so the chamber of tortures became a kitchen, and from the kitchen there pranced new culinary delights. They were sprinkled with the spice of fear, but it was a fiery taste I was learning to enjoy. It all happened slowly. If an outsider read my proud list of progress out loud, they couldn't understand that I was really making changes. But to those that did, my sense of achievement was echoed in the glee that glowed from my family, Sam, my friends, Vicki and Louise. Or, rather, it was their reflections that made, allowed, me to feel good about myself – that cast still needed to crack.

My first outing after seeing both Vicki and Louise was to a salad bar in Piccadilly with Sam. This was where I was going to put the new philosophy into practice and implement my fresh nutritional guidelines too. It was one of those places where you grab a bowl and then pick and choose from a wide selection of ingredients all displayed colourfully in a booth. Here there were bartenders behind the counter and we could select an amount of garnish, which was then arranged in a bowl and handed over with a smile. I began my medley with a few lettuce leaves, followed by all sorts of raw crunchy vegetables not sitting in any daunting sauce. I proudly added a spoonful of kidney beans having made sure they had not been adulterated either and finally asked whether the steamed broccoli had any oil or butter on it, to which the answer was a reassuring 'absolutely nothing at all'. I made my way merrily to the till and sat opposite Sam in a bright green plastic chair. He was happy, I was happy; it had all gone smoothly.

I enjoyed a mouthful of kidney beans, which really was astounding, followed by a trio of pepper shavings, orange, yellow and red. Then I pricked my fork into a leafy broccoli floret and munched at it, still cheerful, but then the smile dropped. My piece of broccoli had olive oil on it, and that was not part of the deal. They had promised me that there was nothing on the broccoli, no oil, no butter, 'nothing at all'. And now I had swallowed, and now I was feeling a flush of red rushing to my cheeks. I felt faint. Sam tried to talk me through it, but this was no time for rational thought. With eyes full of tears I explained to the staff that their *lie* was utterly out of order and that they had better know a little more about their produce before selling it to customers under a dishonest name. But I did sit back down, and I did finish off the rest of my salad, having carefully removed all trace of broccoli out of my bowl and into Sam's.

We walked out holding hands, dejected, saddened. But we still managed to enjoy the rest of a sunny afternoon in London. We would not be disheartened by so little and were not about to give up without a fight.

I reported the incident to Louise at my session with her the following week. I trembled at the thought of all the words of reproach that she would inevitably flip at me from her side of the room, and all the belittling criticism she was likely to fling at me from her comfy leather chair. That was, after all, the way things had worked in therapy up until now. So I spoke with caution but did not miss out a detail. And to that her reply: 'You know what? It's *okay*.'

I felt myself sink into my seat, letting out a long sigh of relief at what I had just heard. And while I held an imaginary whip in one hand, ready to lash another thrashing at my flank, she commended me for sitting through the rest of my lunch and not walking out. She extolled my 'grown-up' behaviour in having dealt with the initial shock upon tasting a glaze of oil, then saying out loud what was going wrong, then letting off some steam and finding a solution that allowed me to stay there, with Sam, till we had both (nearly) finished our plates. So I hadn't managed to eat the broccoli that time. Perhaps that was still a step too far beyond the comfort zone? And maybe next time I would astonish myself with a little more strength, enough to brave that extra stride. But, for now, I needed to give myself a break and put the beating belt to rest.

15

The healing process had begun, and I, as before, was eager to give it my very best shot. Twice a week, on the Oxford Tube, down to London for my therapy. It was exhausting to manage the time I had to take out of university and to tweak my frame of mind, both on the way in and coming back out, to match the two different scenes. And while on the one hand I was so ready, eager, motivated to take on this brand new curative approach that felt so right and made me feel so hopeful, yet I was also riddled with a new kind of fear that I had never experienced (or acknowledged) before. I had previously always been afraid of anorexia and felt a victimised bird in desperate need for someone to deliver me from my cage. Now, I was just as, if not more, afraid of *getting better* than I was of being ill. The fiend had finally managed to make herself my friend. It felt safe in this cage and I was not sure that I was ready for the great big world lurking round the corner. My final year of university was to see me hit rock bottom before I could eventually emerge stronger than ever before. My disease took a dimension so powerful that I was alien to myself, unrecognisable in my behaviour too.

25 October 2003 (aged 20)

There is such a discrepancy between my body and mind – more so than ever before. Spiritually, I feel so much more 'elevated', yet physically I know that I am reduced to a ghostly (ghastly) appearance. Yet I still cannot deal with spending a day without some form of exercise. The more exercise I can do, the better I feel inside and the easier it is for me to eat. Otherwise I have the sensation that my body is simply stocking up tissues of fat and I sense an uncomfortable 'cushioning' effect in my thighs. What I want is to build muscle and tone. And yet it is all so strangely superficial of me and not like anything I ever felt before. I am crawling in my skin like never before. And at the same time when I see curvy women in the street I am envious of their feminine shape and wish I could go back to being that way. I wish I could just snap my fingers and reach my target, but it is the reaching of it that is so exhausting.

My college had no room to offer in-house accommodation to third-year students. We were to arrange our own lodgings, sharing generally with one or more friends. Olivia, my best friend from school, was at a university in Oxford, too, and although she was not at the same college, we decided to move in together just as we had always said we would when we were little girls. Here was a dream come true: independence, freedom, my own front door, my kitchen stocked with any food of choice. We took photos of our first homemade dinner: two girls with radiant smiles and a plateful of steamed vegetables. Except hers was drizzled with olive oil, complemented with a piece of bread and finished with a chocolate bar. Mine kept to its pure, virtuous, form, and may have ended with a piece of gum.

From there on my recollection of that year comes and goes in a kaleidoscopic display of cloudy flashbacks. We didn't have a dishwasher, so I bought my own scrubbing brush and labelled it with a sticky tag so it would only be used for my mugs – and so my mugs would not run the risk of cross contamination from a plate that may have been doused in grease. I also cunningly marked my cutlery with a knife and hid it towards the back of the drawer so that, again, I could control the hazard of my knife, fork or spoon coming in contact with any danger foods AND then being scoured with the wrong brush. How hard it must have been for Olivia to live with a ghost. How she must have wondered where her friend had disappeared to. How much she must have loathed Cruella for stealing me from her – for robbing her of the fun that she was meant to have in the flat shared with her very best friend. Was she in fact still able to discern between Cruella and me? I cannot imagine; I do not know.

I had a pair of socks for bed to keep me warm at night. I got cold and often woke up in the morning with cramps, just as before. I had a separate pair of socks to wear in my slippers to walk from my bed to anywhere around the house. We had a cleaning lady come once a week, a 'shoes-off' policy and both had a keen sense of hygiene. And yet the thought of what might be lurking in the carpet and may then come creeping from my feet to my bed meant that I had to cover my feet at all times. But the only creeping bug was that of an obsession branching out into others.

Sam was asked to clean his feet before going to bed; and any suggestion from him that I was developing a compulsive disorder was met with a condescending sneer and the warning that his own standards of hygiene had better change if we were ever to consider sharing a flat one day. When I went to his house, which was shared with five other friends, I would bring my own mug and always kept a stack of plastic plates and spoons in his room.

Days grew shorter and the weather colder. We lived at the very end of Oxford and it was a bus ride, cycle or walk to get to lectures. I chose the latter two, always, come rain or shine – and most days it was rain.

I felt myself shrinking, and sinking ever deeper through a hypnotic spiral that had taken narcotic dimensions I had never experienced before. My days all matched a set template that involved waking up early, cycling to class, Marks & Spencer apples and pears, chosen with so much care, each inspected to make sure I had selected the 'best'. Then cycling to lectures, Starbucks decaf coffee with Sam, cycling home via Tesco's, spending a painstaking amount of time discovering new forbidden temptations stacked neatly on the shelf and scrutinising the remaining safe options with a scientifically accurate mental calorie counter, ticking away, crunching numbers so I could make my way to the till in peace.

I'll always remember the day I was waiting in a queue, a basket full of vegetables, apples, pears, fat-free yoghurt and herbal tea, and the man standing in front turned to look at me with sorry eyes. He spoke with a foreign accent (or perhaps that is the way I remember his voice) and said in the most soft-spoken way that my basket ought to be more full, or fuller of more filling food. I froze, cold already as

I was, and replied politely that I was fine, actually, thank-you-very-much.

I wonder whether I will ever come to do the same one day. There is a woman at my gym who is twice my age. She dresses a body made of grey flesh and bone with a tracksuit revealing too many pointy joints darting through her clothes. Her eyes bulge and her cheekbones protrude like an organic winter squash. She walks around with that single-minded determination I know all too well. I look at her and want desperately to hold out my hand. And yet I know that I didn't want that sort of charity or help from random people in the street. I know I hated the glances and the glares; I hated the sense of being watched with unforgiving stares, pitied like a starving prisoner of war, judged because nobody understood. I came to grow eyes on the back of my head.

And who am I to claim to know what she is going through or that my shoulder could offer any support? I hated it when we were all thrown into the same basket, like eggs, except handled with less care. I still do. So I decide to leave her alone and only ever to look at her with fleeting eyes, as I would anyone else when my mind wanders away from the treadmill. It's strange to be the observer this time; it feels odd sitting on this side of the fence.

But I want to return to year three. That was the year of the phoenix.

I was seeing Louise and Vicki, each, weekly. That meant hopping on a bus down to London, generally on two separate days as they were both so busy and found it hard to coordinate time-slots. These sessions were helping, every time a little more. But it was still moving slowly. It was tougher than ever before. The Devil had befriended me and dragged me all the way down to the bottom of her hellhole. She had managed to creep right under my skin this time. We had to extricate her with tweezers, the witch.

It crept up on me like the spider spinning its web. I found myself mesmerised by her twisted ways and soon I would be walking the plank. I started taking a picnic with me to class: one big sandwich bag without a sandwich. I would steam my vegetables in the morning then line them on a plate so they might cool before I stuffed them in the bag; one Ryvita or a rice-cake, and an apple for a treat. This was not food to be shared nor were mealtimes a social break. By lunch I was so hungry that I could barely think straight and any excuse was good enough to run off, away from chirpy students, far from any offer to 'grab a bite' – away and to a corner where I could indulge in my ration, in peace.

Sometimes I met with Sam and we shared a pack of prawns with salad. I would have eight, he would try to tempt me to eat more, I would refuse. Again, I would choose the very end of an empty table to minimise the chance of being surrounded. And I felt harassed when friends came to join us, pestered when they looked into my plate and assaulted when they boldly offered kind words about how healthy our food looked compared to their own. I needed to eat in calm and quiet surroundings, with no frivolous distraction; it was a sacramental time that deserved to be treated with respect. Otherwise I would not digest my food.

Everything I did was done with ritual rigour and required a quiet, unperturbed space in which to practise with care. The way I cut my fruit, apples and pears after dinner such that the segments were neither too chunky nor too small. The way I warmed those segments over my great big mug of tea since they came straight out of the fridge (so they would keep the very same rock-hard texture as they had when I meticulously chose them from the store).

The time I took in supermarkets to browse through every produce and product; to check labels, inspect packaging and ultimately select the 'very best' from laundry liquid to yoghurt, fruit, vegetables, even magazines. The same applied in other shops where I generally tried on three or four identical items in matching sizes just to find the one that fitted best.

There is still, to this day, an unfathomable need for everything I touch to be 'just right'. I will scrutinise every white plate from a pile of twenty or more until I find the one with the finest shape, no scratch, no fingerprints and not a score. I will compare bottles of water to make sure mine is most full of all and that the plastic is not dented anywhere. I will undo a neat display of chicken breasts to find the package at the very back with the freshest date and looking 'cleanest' of the lot. And so it goes on. And it is mentally exhausting. Only the other day I was in a stationery shop with my six-year-old niece to buy her stickers, and a notebook for me to have everywhere I go, in which to write this book of mine. I started ploughing through the organised stack placing one pad next to the other, checking every cover and binding to find the most intact. I decided to ask Cecilia to choose for me: that would make it 'special' and I thought she might find it fun to choose 'the very best of them all'. Puzzled, she looked at me and answered in the purest voice of a bamboozled little girl: 'But, Emily, they are *all* exactly the same!' I had been put back in my place and just then I was the child.

I never totally stopped eating. It was more a discipline of 'health' taken to dangerous extremes. The foods I cut out could almost be justified by articles in the 'well-being' sections of the press. But it was a detox taken much too far and dragged out so long that it became a way of life – then death.

I became more angry, more anxious, thin-skinned: tired. As days went by, so the blinkers closed in and soon it was a dark shadow where I was walking, and soon I was the shadow; I was a shadow of myself.

My physical relationship with Sam had come to a natural halt as I was gradually removed from the body that I was no longer able to distinguish as mine. I became more and more disgusted with what mirrors reflected back at me. I did *not* think I was too fat; quite the contrary. There was a skeleton peering at me from behind the looking glass and all I could recognise were those two eyes that change colour with the weather; right now they were grey. It was impossible for me to give myself to Sam when I had next to nothing to give and hated what little I had left. Until then I had never realised how much loving another involved loving one's self; and to feel loved also involves knowing that the person you love is able to receive, and accept, such tenderness.

We slept in separate rooms. Making love hurt. Not only because I was in no way connected to any sense of enjoyment, but also, purely, because I was just too frail. It felt invasive to be touched and almost repellant to go any further than a kiss. Occasionally I would lie back, stare at the ceiling and do what I could to pleasure Sam in a vague attempt to save our relationship. But it was ugly prostitution and Sam deserved so much more. Yet he never gave up on me and continued to stand by my side. I was mean, cutting and dry. I sometimes projected my own self-revulsion on to him. Yet he was still able to hear beyond that voice that wasn't mine and see that the girl he loved was momentarily trapped in this ghastly corpse. It was unquestioning love, not martyrdom. To this day he has never held me to it; never even suggested that I might 'owe' him anything in return. It was in his eyes that I began to remember myself.

There is a sordid side of me that wishes someone had taken pictures of me naked at the time because those are haunting images that I can never allow to fade. I believe it is important to have stark reminders near at hand: diary entries, photographs, even external accounts of what it was like. As people, we have an exceptional capacity to filter through the bad and hold on only to the good in order to move forward, holding our heads high. I want to keep hold of the great and let it shine, but I also want to be able to visit the grim, as my safeguard.

16

By the end of term one of my third year I went home for Christmas. It is one of the most vivid memories that comes still to haunt me when I expect it least. By Christmas I was no longer angry, not nervous, less anxious, still sad and thin-skinned, but mostly I was numb. Feeling required too much energy and I had none to spare. I simply floated on a cloud of seeming inner peace and all surrounding events passed me by without a blink. Illumination is the first word that springs to mind; it was the light of which they speak when death looms round the corner. My illumination was due to a state of utter exhaustion: it was not that I had reached such spiritual heights as to claim attaining new levels of understanding; no new heights of wisdom. I was drained of any strength to laugh. That is what I remember most. How incapable I was of laughing, less because I had lost a sense of humour, more because I had no strength in me to summon up a smile.

Smiling pulled at my face where the skin had lost its

elasticity and stretch. It gave me wrinkles and felt tight. My whole body felt covered in dried-out mud, arid and stiff. Pointed joints protruded from my body and sitting for too long gave me cramps. I remember going to watch the third *Lord of the Rings* film at the cinema with my brother and parents. I had a little plastic bag with a yoghurt and a spoon from home to keep me going. I only emptied half the pot but filled the rest with my napkin and neatly placed it all back in its bag. By the end of the film my whole body ached and it felt as though my bones had pierced through the seat. Three hours was too long, even in a padded chair. Taking baths hurt too much and I had to suspend myself in the water with my arms in order to relieve my backside from the solid tub. Yet I always wanted a bath, sometimes more than once in the day, because that was the only way to keep me warm.

I was cold. My hands were cold. My head felt so cold. My eyes were cold. My heart suffered from cold. Hot drinks and baths were the only way to warm me up. I remained clutched all day to an extra-large mug, barely able to think straight because of the cold. After eating I felt the cold rush to my head, as if my body could not summon the energy to warm me up *and* digest my food at the same time. My digestion was sluggish anyway. I still easily get cold and it still sometimes creeps into my bones. And when that happens I need a mirror held to my face for reassurance that I am no longer ill. I hate the cold. It makes me feel sad.

When I cried it was more that tears spontaneously trickled from my eyes. Not an action, more an effortless automatic response triggered nearly every day. That was one emotional outlet that has never stopped.

We were all sitting down for dinner; my brother had just arrived from New York, but my sister had not yet arrived home. The sound of cutlery clinking against our plates filled the room with a constant reminder of that which was not said. Then, for the first time, I let out a sigh that turned into a tear and my hands came to pillow my cheek as I rested my head against the dinner table and whispered, 'I cannot go on.'

I think back and it sends shivers down my spine. I remember the scene as clearly as I would a passage in a film. It is the same level of reality. Images that mark me and remain engrained in my mind; characters with whom I can relate, but from a distance. I see a little girl crashing and while her heart may still be pumping, every beat is an effort and every effort one too many for a body that 'couldn't go on'. It makes me sad. Those words, that gesture, the puppet momentarily let loose of the chains that dangled her around. A rag doll.

On first impression these are the lines of a closing act. And yet the truth is that just then I had seized the tools of resolution and right there I had made the decision to live. I was surrendering the rag doll to those who loved her most so that they could stitch me up with patches of love leaving no room eventually for evil things to rip at the seams.

My brother, my mother and I, together, began to draw a plan of action with clear steps to recovery and sturdy crutches to help me walk the way. I didn't think I could face going back to Oxford.

25 December 2003

Here is the point. If I think of what comes after university, I feel excited and encouraged. However, whenever I think of a nearer future, whenever I stop to remind myself that before following my dreams I must finish Oxford and sit exams, then I simply feel sick and all the tightness comes back inside. When this happens, all I want is the comfort, cosiness and love of home. In three weeks I am due to fly back and I think I hear a voice deep down holding me here. I just cannot deal with the thought of all that anymore. I have had enough and just want to move on to something fresh and new. Oxford feels stale. But I also know that I might hate myself one day if I let everything go so close to the finishing line. I know as well that this could then become symptomatic; that there is a real risk that I might turn into a 'touche-à-tout', dipping into everything here and there but never really bringing anything to term – for fear of failing?

Why am I so sickened at the thought of having to pull through? Is it because I really no longer can manage? Is it because I cannot deal with the pressure? And if I do not believe I can deal with the pressure, then why do I feel that way? Because I do not think I am – I do not feel – adequate, nor really capable. Nobody is pressing for me to get a First. All they want is for me to be happy. I myself know how frivolous and ephemeral grades and marks are. I know what little value that number on a piece of paper will have on the grand scale of things. And yet I also want to give it my very best. But my very best is exhausted and has had enough.

It is utterly absurd when I think how much my whole life is defined – and controlled – by numbers, as though they are the only real thing to which I can cling; as though they are the only quantifiable measure of my worth:

weight
calories
kilos
grams
distance travelled on foot

hours till my next meal
marks on my essays
grades in my exams
time past
time going by
time to come

I want to be active; *I want to give; I am sick and tired of
the surreal bubble that is university, where we become so
absorbed in ourselves and with our books.*

I love my friends
I love my family
I love my Sam

But I do not understand why they all continue to love me.

My pretext was that it all seemed so pointless; that the
burden was so heavy and my shoulders so frail that I simply
could not do it. My family talked it through with me and
ultimately the choice was mine, but I was reminded also of
how happy my friends made me feel, how important it was
to see things through, that the grades and the workload
should be taken with a pinch of salt and that I should

approach it all with much more lightness in my attitude. How important also for my sense of self-worth, not that it was determined by a university diploma, but that it could only be re-enforced (or put into force) by the feeling of accomplishment, closure, one door shut while so many others opened up. I decided to go back.

I already had Vicki and Louise, the one with directions to nourish my body with fuel, the other with guidelines to feed my soul with care. Now we needed to find a way to put their theories to practice: I needed a helping hand. Short of being hospitalised, bed-ridden and force-fed, we needed to find a way to get me eating real food without the hassle of preparation. Any excuse was good enough for me not to pull out pots and pans, and when I did, through chopping, mincing, boiling and washing up, I had too much time to think, and measure, and calculate, and filter through, eliminate – it was a rigorous ritual that kept me paddling through cement.

My grandmother lived a fifteen-minute drive from Oxford city centre. She had room, a comfortable bed, quiet setting, people there to look after her and cook her food every day – three times a day, or more if required. This was a set-up similar to that which I had in Geneva, except this time my parents would act neither as doctor nor nurse and so that relationship would preserve its healthy distance while remaining bound by unbreakable ties of love. I would carry on through my final year, along with all my friends.

This was key to building my self-esteem, my sense of worth; vital to any option of recovering steps. I would be cared for in a cosy house, in the warmth and safety of my grandmother's home. She is the most forward-thinking, sensitive, intelligent, noble and generous soul I know, and I adore her. Being with her, hearing her talk with the accent of time and the pitch of a life lived long and well, fill me with sparks of inspiration. Her eyes, that deep blue, intensely compassionate and perceptive, piercing through so deep in fact that sometimes I prefer to avoid her gaze. But her eyes, they sweep me away, every time I look into them, every time she looks at me; they are the eyes of wisdom profound and I hope mine will one day shine the same.

Here I was again surrounded by a thick layer of unconditional love; padding that would bounce me back to standing whenever I might stumble and fall.

I first spent half my time living there and the other half still down at the flat, dropped off with boxes full of home-cooked food and all the things I was willing to eat in quantities no longer limited by calorific counts. I was relieved from my thinking duties and given a chance to let go. Slowly slowly the rope loosened enough that I could swallow without a gulp. The food slipped down effortlessly and every mouthful tasted good.

It was working!

17

After four months of my seeing Louise, my parents agreed to attend a 'weekend therapy workshop' recommended – and also attended – by her. As my brother was in America and my sister was busy with children and issues of her own, we decided just the three of us would go. I think that was a mistake. I think we would have benefited enormously from going as a family. I hate that the unit was split.

The idea of this workshop was for people to enter a 'circle of trust' and learn to express sentiments – of hurt, anger, grief, but also love, thankfulness, appreciation – in ways that would serve to re-establish healthy boundaries in all relationships – including those with yourself – to acquire positive communication skills.

We entered the hotel room with the silent consensus that none of us wanted to be there and having made an unspoken pact that we could walk out at any point in time should it all turn out to be a money-grabbing masquerade. Nobody said so; I was too full of hopeful expectations while not so sure what I was hoping to expect. My parents were eager to do anything they could to help and learn new ways – better ways? – of offering support.

My father, a natural-born cynic, held fast to a shield of scientific methodical thinking throughout the weekend. But I could hear beyond the professor's speech, through to the voice of a concerned and loving father and his words pierced straight through to my heart. I knew that this was not safe territory for him and so he simply guarded himself – his family – with the language of reason. But it upset me to think that the rest of the group would receive his darts of logic with the impression that he was a cold and steely man. He is not. And I should know better than to worry about what others think, how they may judge. I should know better than to lose sleep over someone's glance or someone else's murmur. This is something I am still trying to learn.

I am bound by oath not to talk about the group and I cannot describe in too much detail how it all worked either. But I can set the scene and I will tell the results those three days yielded.

We walked into a room set with chairs placed in a circle. All around were scattered boxes of tissues waiting patiently to be put to use. As the room began to fill, everyone found their place within the circle, at first a little awkwardly sat, but soon fastened to their chairs with safety belts all buckled up. Wandering eyes travelled timidly around the room. Uncertain smiles tentatively reaching out. Feet tapping nervously on the floor, hands fiddling with loose jewellery, fingers holding pens wishful that with a touch of magic they might miraculously turn into cigarettes. We were all given a folder, then asked to present ourselves with a name and a 'blurb', followed by the pledge that this was now a circle bound in trust and nothing could ever leak from the bond that was about to form.

It was a melting pot of pain. People were there for reasons ranging from alcohol addiction to suicidal tendencies, from bereaved daughter to a couple on the brink of divorce and then there was me, the youngest in our group, the only one suffering from anorexia. But pain was our common thread.

Day one was mostly an introduction, training us to think in a certain way, or rather to deactivate thinking and let the heart speak for itself. We were given a crash course on how to tap into 'core feelings' and boil any singled-out event or typical occurrence down to a few simple words, meaningfully unadorned. We walked out that night with the strange sensation of something shaking inside. Like tired nerves from head to feet there was a trembling that would not stop. We were asked not to discuss what had happened that day, just to let it sink in without seeking intellectual reassurance.

On the second day we all found our spot and each respected where the other's space began. Around coffee, biscuits and tea, we all began to chat, drawn to those faces that somehow fitted our own. Soon there was the sense of camaraderie and the room was now a web of tissues being passed round, hands reaching out and smiles unleashed without reserve. Turn by turn they took to the floor and were stripped bare before our eyes, exposing a naked soul, so vulnerable, yet safe in the shelter of our man-made fort of trust.

But my family asked for a separate stage.

My parents would not share our story with the rest. And I was too afraid that the room would turn into a tribunal with our group the jury and my parents put on trial. I could not handle the guilt and I could not deal with misconceived blame. My father was willing to play the game so long as it did not involve putting any of his own cards on the table. My mother was held back by a language barrier, unable to express herself fully in English and unwilling, as always, to speak any English at all in front of my father.

I regret to this day that we were allowed to have our own private session, though I am sure it was probably the only way to get my parents to participate fully and I am not sure that I was equipped with the tools necessary to say what I wanted to say in front of everyone else. Already I was so worried about offending anyone and I also desperately wanted to cajole, cushion and ultimately to *please* my parents still. And yet, still, we were thieves. We came in and stole from the group a little courage. We were an audience to their acts and then performed our own play behind a curtain tightly closed. It belonged too much to the family trait that never quite conformed and always sought the best of all worlds; the 'best' of everything.

We were each sat in a chair, in the middle of a bleak conference room, away from everyone else.

The workshop involved teaching us to express our own perception of any given relationship, be it with others or with ourselves, in a way that bore neither blame nor shame. Singular events and specific moments in time were selected to illustrate how certain patterns of behaviour might affect us. First, we would start by listing positive features and the happy feelings they engendered. These were followed by the same number of 'negative' points that were so much more difficult to read out loud.

'When you … Like the time … It makes me feel …'

Finally, in closing, we were taught to set 'boundaries' and to learn to accept that while we cannot change the way others behave, we can draw a clear line where such behaviour affects us in ways more harmful than good.

Simple phrases: 'Next time you … I will first ask you to stop, and if you continue I will protect myself by walking out of the room/hanging up the phone …'

It all seems so childish and utterly lacking in sophistication when discussed from a cautious distance. But in fact very few people know how to articulate their feelings without the defensive tone of reproach or apologetic undertones of remorse. It is not so easy to approach sensitive topics in a way that fully relieves us of a burden without passing on the load to someone else. These are tools of communication with which we all should be supplied. What once would have been a bellow full of accusation and fingers darted in the air could now turn into a calm address where the focus is turned on matters of perception; 'when you ... it makes me feel ...', the implication being 'this is how *I* pick up on such behaviour and I need you to know that while I cannot expect you to alter your ways, I will now do what I can to take care of myself by removing myself from an unhealthy situation'. Uncomplicated, undemanding, light.

What struck me most throughout our session, and with all the others too, was that the real emotional meltdown, every time, came when the list of positive attributes was read. And how, with no exception, there came the line 'when you look after yourself ... like the time ... it makes me feel happy, hopeful, *loved*'. That far from being described as selfish or egocentric, the act of tending to one's own needs and nurturing one's own spirit actually touches the ones we love.

Perfect

Here is what my mother wrote to me in our workshop:

List of concerns/confrontations:

1. Emily, when you continue to lose weight, I feel **fear** and **sad**

2. Emily, when you hide away from me, I feel **sad**, **lonely** and **fear**

3. Emily, when you think too much instead of just letting go and allowing yourself to live, I feel **sad**

4. Emily, when you are suspicious in restaurants or distrustful at home (olive oil etc.), I feel **anger**

5. Emily, when you push back opportunities to try food you always loved, that is good, healthy and home-cooked, I feel **fear**, **sad** and **anger**

List of appreciations:

1. Emily, when you take care of yourself (with help from Vicki and Louise), I feel **happy**, **grateful**, **hopeful** and **peaceful**

2. Emily, when you are happy with Sam, Olivia and your friends, I feel **happy**

3. Emily, when you summoned the courage to go back to Oxford I felt **happy**, **hopeful** and **relieved**

4. Emily, when you bought yourself a bottle of extra virgin, top-quality olive oil you chose on your own

and that you *enjoy* a little every day, I feel **happy** and
very hopeful

5. Emily, when we laugh together, I feel **very happy**
6. Emily, when you put your recovery into action, I feel
   hopeful and **grateful**

Goals/commitments:

- What I will do to help build a healthier relationship:
  I will trust you more and ask fewer questions of you.
  And I will no longer weigh down on you with my own
  anxieties.
- What I will do for my recovery:
  I will continue to be the mother that I am, but I will
  pay more attention to my husband and to myself so
  that I can communicate more strength and joyfulness
  on to you all.
- Something special I will do for myself is:
  To spend more time with my friends and develop new
  interests.

And at the bottom of the page, she added (though this was
not part of the exercise!):

> *Spontaneous comments*: I probably understood
> nothing of what we were supposed to do and got
> this thing all wrong and I probably haven't totally

got my head around drawing up boundaries but I love you. And thank you for allowing us to share such intensely positive moments with you. xx

Maman

Here is an excerpt of what I wrote to my mother:

List of concerns/confrontations:

1. Maman, when you want to be the one to 'fix' me, I feel **shame** and **guilt**
2. Maman, when you say you are tired/worn out/cannot sleep, I feel **guilt, anger, shame, hurt, lonely** and **sad**
3. Maman, when you 'know best', I feel **anger** and **hurt**
4. Maman, when you are angry, sad or hurt, I feel **anger, sad** and **hurt**

List of appreciations:

1. Maman, when you encourage me and are positive, like in all your sweet postcards and letters and notes, I feel **loved, relieved, peaceful, happy, proud, grateful** – but also **guilt** and **shame**
2. Maman, when you understand me and say it's okay, I feel **loved, relieved, peaceful, happy, grateful** – but some **shame** and **guilt**
3. Maman, when you support and encourage me, I feel

loved, **relieved**, **peaceful**, **happy**, **grateful** – but also
guilt and **shame**

4. Maman, when we laugh together, I feel **loved**, **happy**,
relieved, **peaceful**

5. Maman, when you kiss me and take me in your arms,
I feel **loved**, **peaceful**, **hopeful**, **happy** and **relieved**

6. Maman, when you take care of yourself, I feel **happy**,
relieved and **hopeful**

7. Maman, when you are happy, peaceful, hopeful, I feel
happy, **peaceful**, **hopeful**

Goals/commitments:

- What I will do to help build a healthier relationship:
I will tell you when and why certain of your behaviours
impact on me more than you know, but above all what
emotional effect they have on me instead of just
keeping it all inside of a great big lump in my throat
and not saying anything at all just to protect you.

- What I will do for my recovery:
I will continue to work on eating better, and more.

- Something special I will do for myself:
I will treat myself to a magical, healthy, holiday with
you!

What became crystal clear to me through the workshop was how desperate I was to protect my parents, and how much they felt the need to protect me too. And how my father always set out to protect my mother and I, in turn, wanted to protect him from protecting her and her from any offence that I might cause. And meanwhile that I needed, so much, to break away from this triangle, to start taking care of myself and let them take care of each other. It was time for me to let go, to push my chair back and leave theirs at close proximity to one another. It was about understanding that no matter how great a *physical* distance there naturally came in time between my parents and me, we would always be there for each other and continue to love each other just as much, only with healthier boundaries to act as props.

When I stop to think about where this deep sense of responsibility came from, this duty to protect, I am beginning to see that it all took root in the little girl who wanted so much to please. It all stems back to that fear of disappointing, the dread of letting other people down. It was less about protection and more about perfection. I was projecting my own voices, my own anxieties and insecurities on to them and creating, in my head, another set of parents to the couple sat in front of me who loved me no matter what. They were not telling me to be better than best; in their eyes I was never insignificant nor ever made to feel worthless. They asked of me one thing only: to be happy. They wanted to see me fulfilled in whatever I chose to do with my life, but above all just to live and let go. And yet, I wanted above all to be happy for them and the choices I made – still very often today – were driven almost entirely by their points of view: but why? I just don't know.

I remember when my parents put me on the Oxford Tube to go back to university and waved goodbye, trying so hard to put on a brave face. But their apprehension glimmered from the back of their eyes and I could tell how sick they felt to see me ride away so sickened still. It was a Sunday evening; two buses zoomed by without stopping because they were jam-packed. Then my bus pulled over and I stepped nervously inside. I scrambled on to the upper deck and struggled over luggage dumped in the passageway to the very back where a man kept dropping his slumbering head on my brittle shoulder. There were droplets of sweat steaming in condensation on the windows. I felt so small, and lonely.

My mother, I later learned, was deeply disturbed by what she witnessed at the workshop. So much more than I ever realised at the time. I thought that the weekend had revealed things that would build healthier pathways between the three of us. It had been hard but ultimately cathartic, I believed. There was an atmosphere that no words can describe, surreal almost, bizarre at times, that had affected us all in a weird, dream-like way and we hadn't really been given the chance to snap out of it before stepping back outside. For my mother, it was a nightmare. All the sadness she heard, all the despondency she saw, all of it she had sopped up like a sponge. Now someone needed to wring the sponge dry. I was too immersed in my own circle of hell at the time for any surrounding misery to drag me further down. But that weekend yanked my mother back to another slump. I didn't know at first, but I found out the next time I went home, and it made me feel sad, upset, helpless again. The wheel just kept on turning.

The Monday morning after our workshop I called Louise in tears. I felt so vulnerable, breakable, weak. There was a powerful circle of trust that had shielded us from reality over the weekend. It was beginning to feel so safe in that room. And it had all been so, so intense without enough time for closure. I needed some kind of closure. I needed to know that whatever abscess had been burst was now going to heal, not to continue oozing with all the scary things that had been kept shut inside. I wanted my parents, I wanted Louise, I wanted the blankets and all the curtains shut.

Louise listened and heard. She put me face to face with the little girl that felt afraid and asked me then to take care of her like only I knew how. That was what I needed to do. I needed to do something for myself. It could be as simple as going out to buy sweet-smelling soaps and running myself a bath. Or going for a stroll in the sun, looking at the trees, reconnecting with the world that could be so beautiful if we took the time to look at it properly. I felt more calm when I hung up and drew a list of things I wanted to do, for me. I am not sure whether any of it was put into practice there and then, because I had not yet quite reached full capacity to take care of myself and give myself a real break, but the list gave me hope and told me of all the possibilities that could be opened up with the great big key of uncertainty.

18

I began to revise for finals and I was afraid. There was a weight pressing down on my not-so-sturdy frame. Every day I wanted to throw my notes to the flames and put my ink to better use. I wondered about the point of it all and questioned why we put ourselves through such remarkable anguish for the sake of a few scribbles on a page and marks based on a contrived set of archaic rules which would place us in a box, carefully labelled, placing geometric limits on our young and candid aspirations. It didn't seem right.

One afternoon stands out in my memory of the time. I am often asked whether I can put my finger on a 'turning point'; what it was that suddenly made me change my mind. The truth is that there is no such date and that I didn't so much 'change my mind' as switch to listening to the kinder side of myself. Still, this day was important and stands out like the polished stepping stone.

I had been studying in my room all day. Numbers and

words were dancing in my head to an unnerving beat that was beginning to make it spin. I was swimming through sinking sand. I couldn't do it, I couldn't remember a thing. Four walls closing in on me and nowhere to gasp for breath.

I felt alone.

I called my brother.

I needed to protect my parents; it was the fear of worrying or disappointing them – or a combination of the two. And Patrick always knew what to say and he always knows how to listen. Sometimes all we need is someone to listen and hear us cry out loud, without judgement, just the compassionate silence of the attentive ear.

It all came flowing in a whirlwind of despair, so much anguish travelling through the phone line, across the Atlantic, to the tennis courts at Flushing Meadows. Patrick listened. He spoke few words but the sound of his comforting voice, steady, tender and calm, put my pounding head to rest. I will never forget the feel-good surprise package that followed. It carried two T-shirts from my favourite American clothes shop, one of which had the words '*Wishing You were Here*' printed in blue on its front, a selection of sweet-smelling body products and a little yellow book called *Tomorrow*. My brother knows me well. And everything was bundled up in bubble-wrap, and as I snapped them playfully, so sparkles of love filled my heart with happiness. These little gestures, such genuine thoughts, go so far in making a difference. And that little box made me feel lucky, and loved.

I found myself walking to the supermarket. Hearing my hunger I marched my way up and down the aisles, filling my basket with foods I never had considered even before all this began. Cravings as if expecting a child – how ironic! It seemed that whereas previously my fear in life projected on to my plate and put a stop to my eating in a vain search of some elusive sense of safety, now my new approach was to step up to the challenge, pick out groceries that felt a little scary because they no longer belonged to a routine. I was breaking from the routine; I was looking forward to 'tomorrow'.

Beetroot, baby corn, margarine. Those were the first three 'new' foods I brought home with me that day. It was the beginning of a crusade. From now on every time I felt the world was coming to an end, I would pick up my two feet and hit the road to try something new. And, every time, the thrill of surmounting my fears and the sense of achievement that came with that was one more battle won. I was conquering. It wasn't that I now was reverting to food to fill creepy feelings; it wasn't that I now was 'feeding' emotions where before it was starving them that felt right. It was simply that I had tasted the sweetness of winning over fear; I had taken a leap of faith and the net really had appeared.

Baby steps. I was letting go, but always paradoxically with control. It was like being on an extendable leash. At first I needed weighing scales and various-sized spoons so I could verify, quantify, put a number on the scary food that I was about to overcome. And then, in due course, and without realising that the transition had occurred, I let go of the scales, and the spoons, and empty see-through jars marked with indelible felt-tip pens acting as trustworthy measuring jars. They just went, with *time*.

They were little thrusts outside the comfort zone that I was taking. I knew not to push the boundaries so fast, so far, that the bubble would burst and I would plummet to the ground from vertiginous heights. But every time I heard how happy my parents, my brother, Sam – all the voices of those who cared – were turned every little step into a triumph. It wasn't so much the congratulations but more the sound of a happy voice, the melody of relief tuned to notes of hope. Theirs was a chorus that kept me singing my part.

26 March 2004 (aged 20)

Too much is going on at once in my body, heart, mind and soul and it feels like I am about to burst with thoughts, feelings, emotions; like my vital organs are finding it really difficult to keep up with the pace and keep the blood pumping through.

Suddenly I am feeling the fear and doing it anyway, and it feels very – overwhelmingly – powerful.

Cruella tries to catch me out and puts a lump of fear in my throat, but I fight her with all my might and phrases like 'I think I can, I know I can, come on Emily; just do it – do the thing you think you cannot do'. Silly clichés like writing a cheesy script to my life on big screen. Postcard idioms. But they help.

I suddenly have this indescribable will-power that just switched on out of the blue and it feels like I am on a roll, driven by something unexpected, beyond words. And it's also very frightening.

I am driven by the reactions of my parents and Sam and Vicki and Louise … I am driven by the sunshine my recovery radiates in their eyes and voice. I am driven by these voices, but also for the first time I think my own positive voices are speaking out and being heard.

But I am dead scared that this happy roll will turn into a roller coaster and that I am bound, very soon, to get a huge downer where the fear takes over and I drown under its might. I am also so afraid of what will happen once I have recovered.

Right now the drive is the strength and power of the

recovery process. I face and manage the challenge, and then the 'admiration'; recognition; pride in me that each victory triggers in my parents above all, but everyone else too. But what happens once I have reached the summit? My fear is that slowly, gradually, people will forget the battles; they will forget the war I just won; I will not be noticed really as anything exceptional. I will perhaps not even have the mental faculties I have now in this state.

I hate the pressure of being tended to and the expectation that I should get better. I hate being told what to do and treated like a child, but I am so scared at the thought of no longer being cared for or regarded in that special way ever again.

It also feels lonely because there is no one out there really to share it with. It's that feeling of loneliness that hurts so much inside. But mixed with the sting of fear; afraid of not being special or 'singled out' amongst a great big crowd.

It is so selfish of me to need so badly to be recognised as something special. I am so ashamed and feel so self-centred. I feel guilty too that I am questioning the love I am receiving constantly, daily. And it makes such an egotistical little brat of me to think all the suffering that I am putting them through.

I must promise myself to turn this minus into a plus and shine a light, in turn, once I have it back in me; to return all that I have received, and more.

*I cannot seem to stop writing and yet I must because I
have got to revise. And every time that consideration hits
me I feel afraid, and sick. And then I no longer feel hungry
and it makes me feel like my thighs are just becoming
plump and fat and ugly. Just like that, upon the click of a
negative thought. And I have to fight that and allow the
good voices to hush her away because she is mere evil.*

While my mind had now reached a point where it was
ready – keen – to rediscover old foods and taste new ones
too, yet my body lagged behind and reacted in ways I could
no longer predict. It had been enslaved for too long now; it
was a chaotic mutiny rising up in all directions. I called
them 'allergies' for lack of a better word: itchy prickling
around the mouth and in my fingertips, phlegm in my
throat, 'numbness' on my tongue, runny nose, headaches,
pins and needles. But there was no logical explanation nor
any consistency to the way my body behaved. Sometimes it
was one ingredient, but the next day I could eat a plateful
of that same food and feel fine. My whole digestive system
had dramatically slowed down and on top of having to
spark itself up again it was now having to deal with new
things to break down too.

I remember this strange chilly sensation like a pair of

frozen spectacles around my eyes after eating. The same iciness would settle up my nose and momentarily diminish my capacity to smell. I always needed a hot drink with my food: for a very long time it was the only way to warm up the digestive system and stimulate it into action. And without something warm I felt too tired; not enough energy reserve for keeping me going while processing a meal.

I looked so often like the famished child we see on TV with stick-thin limbs and bulging belly. My stomach protruded because it was filled with air from chewing-gum and sugar-free fizzy drinks. I also had no muscle left there for me to pull it in. It felt uncomfortable and looked pitiful. Whenever I ate or drank anything too acidic my skin would immediately constrict and go dry to the bone. As though by osmosis my body was trying to buffer the acidity in my blood, drawing neutralising water from where it could. I don't know. But it was disagreeable and made it that much harder even just to smile.

The artificial sweeteners I was ingesting on a daily basis through sugar-free drinks, gum, yoghurt, were accumulating inside and messing me up to an alarming degree. It came to a point where I could feel little bubbles travelling down my thighs and in my stomach. These, I was told, were literally the chemicals effervescent in my blood. My knees felt stiff, my hands and elbows tight, I had cramps in my shoulders. This, it was explained to me, was because the body always seeks to protect our vital organs first and so it flushes any toxins away from heart and lungs and towards our less important extremities where they stack up in our joints if there is no fat reserve to store them instead. The sweeteners were toxic

In the last couple of months leading up to my final exams I moved into my grandmother's house full-time. This way I could focus entirely on my revision and my recovery – though by this stage the latter was taking primary importance. No need to shop for food, no need to cook my food, I didn't have to make my bed nor clean my clothes. The house was always warm; fridge and cupboards were full at all times. I had access to my grandmother's car and was granted permission from college to park on campus so that there was no essential energy wasted in travelling to and fro. This all made a dramatic difference and I cannot say for sure that I would have managed to see it through to finals without such a reassuring support mechanism in place. And it was so important for me to be able to see it through to finals somehow. Otherwise I am not sure, either, whether the rest of this story would ever unravel the way it did. It was all about finding the balance between leaving me with enough autonomy to feel positive, self-assured and gradually build up my confidence, all against a backdrop of safety nets, security covers and protective bubble wrap.

My days, from 9 a.m. till 10 p.m., were spent in our

college library. By this stage we all had appropriated ourselves with cubby holes at the very back of the building. There were four of us per table. Sam sat across from me and two other good friends were on the other side. Every once in a while the scratch of a pen, ruffling of papers, clumsy coughs or faint cheeky whispers broke out of this deafening silence and tickled us back to a sense of sanity. As before, and as continues to prove true to this day, it was vital that I should be surrounded by those who loved me most – and that *I* loved most. That we should all be travelling towards an equal end point, albeit on parallel roads, made me feel a part of something bigger. It gave me perspective; long-lost perspective.

Anorexia is an intensely solitary disease. She starts by cutting you off so that you might better concentrate on her rigorous rules; there is little space for frivolities when you are in constant arduous calculation. And even when in the company of others, even when in conversation, still the better part of you is engaged in another, more important, tête-à-tête. Then it is a disease so often misconstrued that you cannot help but feel awfully on your own. When you don't quite understand what is going on yourself, you cannot expect to be able to explain the situation in sufficiently clarifying terms to anyone else. To some, you are shallow, others mistrust your every word, and then there are those who prefer to stay away, for fear of contagion or, perhaps, simply out of fear. And you can't keep up with whoever is left wanting to be your friend because you haven't got the energy to have fun, you haven't got the gusto to let go, your options are determined by what you allow yourself to eat and your hours are entirely governed by a strictly regulated routine. So you feel lonely. Detached from others and disconnected from yourself. When you begin to restore a sense of belonging, then you know that you are on the track to recovery.

In my little corner of the library, hidden between stacks of files and underneath shelves brimming with dusty books, there were Tupperware boxes filled with home-made snacks, there was a lunchbox crammed with a suitable meal, there were boxes full of crackers and shopping bags stashed with fruit. On my desk there was a pencil case, piles of highlighted notes, a few good-luck cards throwing a cheerful smile for me to catch, and a line of tall paper Starbucks cups. My brain needed constantly to be fed and my body continuously required something hot to keep it fuelled. By now I was eating, and my stomach was calling for unpredictable cravings. Having 'lived' off vegetables for the past four years – and having been brought up all my life on fresh daily greens, suddenly I was attracted only to wholemeal bread, bananas, apples, tuna, dark chocolate, muesli bars, cereal, chicken, seaweed, tofu and the odd token *tinned* spinach, French beans, mushrooms or baby corn. The alarm signal that had been ringing for so long was finally resonating in my ear. It was a cry for something substantial, and every bit of it was being consumed on the spot. I never realised how much food the brain needs merely to operate, let alone run at the rate I was currently asking it to perform. Mine was a hungry, famished brain and I was now entirely prepared to give it the nourishment it had wanted for so long. It was guzzling away and leaving no extras to store in reserve. I was biting, nibbling, chewing every thirty minutes, and still it begged for more.

There was, officially, neither eating nor drinking allowed in our library. And although my circumstance was clear enough, still there was a limit to what the kind librarian could permit. So long as my stocks were put out of sight she would play along and act as though the bags had passed unseen. But to the paper cups standing proud and tall on my desk, which was on the aisle, she could not turn a blind eye. I still have the photo of the A4 sign that was thereafter posted in the entrance, on the staircase wall, and again near where we were seated. It read:

'Parts of the upper library are beginning to look like the Queen Lane Coffee House just now (especially, but not exclusively, the desk to the left of the statues). We know that you are going through a stressful time, finalists, but PLEASE DON'T BRING FOOD AND DRINK IN HERE. It's a good idea to take a complete break and sit outside to eat and drink – the fresh air will be good for your brain as well. We don't mind water, as long as it's in bottles with caps.'

It made me laugh back then just as it does today to think that I was being asked, respectfully, not to break time-old rules just because I was struggling to keep my heart beating to a regular pulse. Mine, incidentally, was the 'desk to the left of the statues'.

It had been arranged with the support of our senior tutor that I should sit my exams separately to everyone else, with my own invigilator to supervise. He would stop the clock whenever I needed a break, whenever I had to eat. I could not possibly have sat beside fellow pupils scribbling frantically and trying hard to rack their brains of everything they had stashed in there up until seconds before entering the examination room. Not with the shop-front display of biscuits, tuna sandwiches, energy bars, bananas and other motor-foods that I would arrange neatly on my desk to keep me functional. Not with my hasty munching and hurried crunching almost constantly from start to pens down. So I scribbled, and nibbled, and made it through to the final round.

19

It is impossible to define exactly when I shifted from improvement to actually beginning to heal. I looked forward to finishing my last exam with heightened anticipation. There would be so much relief and I should feel so proud. Yet when I set my pen down and as I gathered my things preparing to walk away, I was swamped with a newfound fear. Suddenly there were no obvious handcuffs nor any clear confining walls. Now I was free to move on and to relish that lack of restriction. It was meant to be a time of bouncing up and down and I was going to prance and hop through wild blossom. Instead all I wanted was to hide under cosy covers and seek comfort in my mother's arms. I wanted to be a little girl more than ever before. Here was a new chapter opening on a fresh blank page, and all I wanted was to skip back to the opening chapters of familiar pages.

My glycaemic levels were constantly fluctuating and I had grown exceedingly sensitive to anything too sweet. I had already learned about the importance of having a bit of protein or fibre to slow down any sugar rush and reduce the speed at which sugars are released into the bloodstream, but now I couldn't even have a piece of fruit after dinner without feeling queasy, shaky and suddenly cold. We began to suspect that I might be 'pre-diabetic' and my blood sugar therefore needed careful monitoring to determine how and when it would peak or plummet. My father, who heads his own laboratory for research in diabetes, brought a special kit back home so that every night I pricked my finger before, during and after dinner to watch how fast my glucose would rise and fall. I became more and more careful about my choice of food combinations and learned mostly through trial and error what worked for me and what did not.

My appetite was still impulsive; the food I craved was still particularly random and odd. I still did not feel like having any fresh vegetables and I couldn't understand why. My daily staple was dried fruit compote with yoghurt and sugar-free muesli. That was what I loved to eat – and I ate a lot of. I had not yet managed to regain a certain 'normality' within my diet, neither in the quality nor in the quantity of what I ate. It would take a while before I found that balance again, and longer yet till I was able to eat of everything, without thinking twice, without my choice being picked out from a selective list of what I considered to be 'safe'. Even today I find it hard to keep varying my meals and not to stick to a limited catalogue of familiar food.

We all drove down to Cornwall after the end of exams, a crew of six university friends for a week of relief, respite and relaxation. I remember stocking up on supplies to stash in the car for fear of there being no stores that sold the stuff I liked. When we arrived and unpacked, my provisions were nowhere to be found. Sam took the hit for all the tears, the fear and anger that ensued. I wasn't sure that I would make it through the week and suddenly felt as though stripped of my weapons of defence. We had to take a boat across to the nearest town in order to find a health-food shop so that I could finally enjoy myself too.

Very few people can understand the importance of these things unless they have lived with anorexia themselves or by someone else's side. Anyone 'normal' would not be so inflexible as to have to carry bags full of daily rations in order to feel safe when travelling within the same country and no more than a car-ride away from home. Any average person would not fly off the handle and behave like a very small child if for some reason those bags were left behind. Yet Sam understood, Sam comforted and reassured me, and Sam looked always to finding the solution that could finally put my mind at rest.

I remember that trip to Cornwall in particular because halfway through our stay I suddenly hungered for a large dish full of steamed vegetables. It was the first time in several months that I had such a recognisable desire after months of bizarre cravings. I felt as excited as when I lost my first tooth. We went to the market and bought carrots, broccoli, green beans, peas and spinach. It was with so much joy that I dipped into every dash of colour on my plate and with a thrill that I delighted in every mouthful. I had learned to appreciate all the flavours that tickled my taste buds and every texture in which they came.

Very slowly, things started to change. And, gradually, I shook my wrists of unwanted shackles. I could read whatever I wanted to read and I could put that book down if it didn't appeal. I could pursue my interests and develop hobbies, and if they didn't suit then I could just as easily go back on to something else. I looked forward to looking forward. If this was what 'growing up' was all about, I now wanted in!

Sam and I went travelling in America for two weeks. I have photos of that holiday framed and fixed up everywhere around my flat, a constant reminder of the pure happiness that bubbled along my veins throughout our stay. I felt calm, relaxed. I felt positive and safe. I felt grounded and even comfortable in my skin. I have discovered recently that visualisation is an awesome tool. It brings you near enough to a meditative state without having to take too much time out nor seclude yourself in a quiet empty room to achieve that peace of mind. When I feel anxious, nervous, a little restless or on edge I picture blissful moments and imagine myself there, walking on balmy-smooth sand, stroked by the silky rays of an afternoon sun. Then, not always, but more often than not, my heart slows its beat and my breath becomes softer. These are little aids that go a long way in pushing you out of daily dips.

6 August 2004 (aged 21)

Things are so much better now. I have put on ten kilos since I left Oxford. But that is not the point, contrary to what all too many out there seem to believe. Of course I needed to put on weight. I am not suggesting otherwise. But I could reach a perfect weight and still be anorexic. I could possibly even maintain a perfect weight for the rest of my life and still drag my anorexia around with me always. That is so important for me to bear in mind. Still, a little more bulk gives me strength required to work things out. Things I was too weak, all over, even to contemplate before. Things like 'growing up'.

I have been thinking a lot lately about what it means to be an 'adult'. When will I actually feel wholly 'adult'? Does one ever, actually, feel 'grown-up'? When I finished school I thought everything would feel so different and many transformations would occur. They did. But I only realise that now, with hindsight, looking back. At the time it all felt utterly anti-climactic.

Finishing finals I thought I would feel a different person altogether; that I would then be submerged with an immense sense of endless freedom. Instead, I was unsettled, filled with anxiety and simply wanting to be left alone in peace and quiet for a while.

I still feel no difference, no real sense of having 'matured'. And yet so much has happened and I have moved so far forwards, in so many respects. Maybe when I move to London and find a job? Then will I begin to feel like an 'adult'?

No. I think nobody feels intrinsically, fundamentally 'adult'.

I feel 'grown-up' around my niece and when I take my nephew in my arms. But I feel like a teenager next to my big sister. And I will always feel like a daughter with my parents. Maybe it's just simply all about 'being', without question, without labels.

So awareness comes from looking back. And as I look back I think of how far I have come. I think of Christmas when I was on the verge of giving up my degree and I wasn't even so sure that I would have the energy to pull me *through the night. I think of all the suffering and anguish caused around me. What I put my family through. What I put Sam through. I think of their love and support and faith in me at all times and I just don't know what I could possibly have done in a previous life to deserve to be blessed with so much good fortune, because I see nothing I have done in this existence that could make me worthy of so many honest smiles. And I am determined to make the most, the best, of it now.*

I moved to London in October and started a course in Asian Art at the British Museum. I felt passionate about the subject and while I was not sure that it was leading to any definite career, this was my chance to soften my skin in the sweet milk of learning, without any scoring, marking, grading, with no tests, assessments, examinations, assignment nor obligation. I hadn't taken a gap year before going to Oxford: this was *my* time to enjoy enjoyment without bounds.

My greatest struggle remained fine-tuning my receptors of hunger and discerning whether I was eating certain foods out of a programmed habit or whether my body was really longing for them. For so long I had stuck to a predetermined daily meal-plan, keeping to a strict schedule and measuring my portions according to a set calorific scheme, that now I needed to decode the system and restore my practice to the rudimentary instincts of a newborn child. And that was not easy.

I did not topple into bulimia and binging, but I was still excessively hungry – or at least I believed so – and mostly towards the latter part of the day, going into the evening. Although I was not depriving myself of food from waking through to teatime, still it felt safer eating when the lights were dimmed and the bustle in the streets was securely shut out behind the tightly fastened entrance door to my home. That was when I felt secure, and once the bolt was double-turned rare were the occasions that I would venture back out again. Today I continue to find going out a challenge. I love to be with friends; I hate being alone. And yet I feel lost and vulnerable when immersed in too big a crowd. I feel anxious and unsettled when plunged into a deep pool of loud noise. Then again, here too, I need to start dismantling my method of thought. I need to stop pre-empting the eventual, potential, possibility that I might, perhaps, feel unhappy at any given social gathering and therefore kindly declining all invitations out of principle. But that is not easy.

So my hunger would grow progressively into sundown, and I was most able to take note of its call by nightfall. My cravings were not yet regular, and carried on yielding to the sweeter end. They did not call for chocolate bars, candy, ice-cream nor ready-made 'stodge': it was always unprocessed sugars, unrefined grains, pure cereals and anything tinned in water with nothing added. But the way I ate was nonetheless causing important drops in my blood sugar levels. My body was not yet ticking to its natural clock and I found it hard not to let it put me down. For months I woke up in sweats around 4 a.m., starving. I would go to the kitchen and have whatever it took to satisfy my want for food, then finally return to bed for half a night's tranquil sleep. I wasn't gorging myself in a sickly way and I would never subsequently make myself sick. It was as if my body was on constant starvation alert and took advantage of my sleep to urge me, subconsciously, to stock up in anticipation of future famines.

I remember a nightmare. I saw myself asleep at the very edge of my bed. And then a silhouette approaching, ghost-like, *skeletal*. That of a girl. I opened my eyes and found myself staring at the phantom. She kept coming nearer and I could not move. I was muted. I could not shout out the agonising horror of it all. I kept on staring, powerless. She continued to move towards me and I suddenly recognised her as the shadow of myself. I was coming face to face with my demon. I woke up struggling for breath, drenched with sweat in the back of my neck, forehead soaked and weeping, folded in two from the hurt of fear in my stomach.

I called my brother. He calmed me down. It was 4 a.m. I was afraid and felt lonely. I eventually fell asleep again and when I next opened my eyes it was daylight. Darkness had been and then it had gone.

But healing was hard. Harder even, at times, than being stuck at the bottom of the pit. Climbing out is more exhausting for sure. You are struggling with new shapes, trying to find your ground; you are in a sort of limbo where it is so hard to distinguish whether you feel bad because you are just having a bad day, just like anyone else, or whether it is still the anorexic twitch. More frightening at times too because once you no longer display any obvious physical signs of being ill, people around you, those who love you most in fact, grow impatient. Because they need to turn the page; they want to see you well, they want to pass over getting better. And you feel lonely because you put on a happy face, to please, to offer peace of mind, and more often than not you really mean it when you smile, but sometimes it is a mask, and you feel lonely for hiding behind it, and then you feel ashamed that you should still be hiding behind it at all.

24 November 2004

It's not over yet. And I feel like I have just been drugged or dragged through a trail of mud, or as though I am watching my life on a movie screen, it all feels so remote and surreal. Sam was going to cook a stir-fry for us and I asked him to make it with no oil. I have had a long day. I am tired. I feel vulnerable. He has just freaked out on me and said that he cannot deal with this anymore and that I had to call Vicki or Louise and that I had to get over this fear of oil when I am so capable of eating so much other stuff and leading a near-normal life. I am simply unable to settle myself down right now and talk myself through a rational understanding of the fact that a teaspoon of oil will not kill me. I feel so drained and sick. Maybe I am just coming down with something. But maybe 'they' were right when 'they' say it never really totally goes away and the more I come to that realisation the more I am absolutely petrified at the thought of the turn my life may have taken in the past five years and for ever more. I just don't know what to do. My head hurts and my stomach aches. It all feels so unreal after so much time of its being okay. I am so, so tired and I just don't know what is going to happen with Sam.

I am doing so much better but I do still find it difficult to measure whether I am eating a lot or too little or what.

I swing from thinking everything is a humungous amount to persuading myself that my mind is just playing tricks and that anyway having starved myself for the past five years the least I can do is to treat myself to a bowl of All-Bran! I do not 'binge' on crap food but I will suddenly have three bowls (not enormous) of cereal and two pitta breads with sugar-free jam. Sam says that is not all that much and that so many people have huge fry-ups or a whole pizza or three brownies once in a while, without punishing themselves or feeling the need to walk halfway round the world to burn it off. Yet I still oscillate between taking great care of myself and then feeling guilty for it. It just continues to be so hard to learn to eat without thinking and enjoying my food without analysing or suffering a sudden sugar-crash, which happens so often. I just want to be perfectly balanced and I am so near yet still too far.

20

In an effort of self-preservation, I suppose, this body of mine was now holding on to whatever it was being fed. Whereas I had been proud to recover my old jeans and slip into dresses that had recently only slipped off, now I was having to shop for bigger sizes and my face mirrored pictures of me at an early pubescent age. I was not happy any more. Reassurance was tossed at me from all directions; I was assured that this was to be expected and would not last longer than a year. But I was more and more unhappy. Sam continued to flatter me, but I couldn't believe him. My parents conceded that I did not look my usual self, but were also confident that this too would pass; I was not.

25 January 2005 (aged 21)

After much trial and error it seems that on days when I have a decent lunch and a lighter dinner, relatively early, those are the nights I haven't woken up with a desperate need to eat. However, I also found that when I am not alone it all goes much more smoothly too. When Sam is by my side I sleep much better. But that should not be my only solution or else we are heading straight for a steep road down to co-dependence.

I just need to get used to the fact that I am no longer the size of a frail-looking little girl. I need to learn to embrace the body of a woman, and all that it entails. This is proving harder to digest – literally – than I originally thought it would. I wanted so much to regain my curves and an attractive shape. But I just wish these things could be programmed on demand. I need to accept myself and move on to bigger (!) things in life. Slowly, I think I am beginning to find equilibrium and balance both in body and soul. But it is so difficult to achieve.

It is still not easy to know whether the hunger is now due to an automatic reflex, an alarm clock I need to learn to switch off, or whether it is genuine because my body is needing something because it is still in active repair mode. I still feel like I am crawling in my skin, uncomfortable. I cannot deal with Sam touching me, especially my tummy. It is not easy. I keep on saying so but it just is not, easy.

Self-worth = 2/20

❦

My weight gain was now affecting my confidence. It made me feel ashamed that such superficial matters should matter so much to me. But they did. I felt puffy on the outside and it swelled my heart with gloom. I lacked energy, I was lethargic, I had recurrent headaches and found it difficult to rise bright and early in the morning. I had recently joined a gym, but I had not yet been there once. My lack of physical strength weighed down on my lazy shoulders and made me feel weak inside. I took a food allergy test and was found to be intolerant to over a dozen foods. The amount of ingredients to which I seemed to react badly suggested that the problem lay more in the overall hypersensitivity of my digestive system than with an actual allergic reaction to any given product on the list. I was told I had 'leaky gut syndrome'. This meant that the permeability of my stomach lining had been affected in such a way that bigger pieces of undigested food were passing through into the bloodstream and causing the body to treat them as foreign, unwanted, agents. The underlying issue was that I was infested with 'candida'. Finally an answer that made sense and to which there appeared to be a clear-cut solution. But it meant cutting out many foods to be in the clear.

In a nutshell, and to explain what comes next, Candidiasis is the common name (though not globally recognised across the scientific field) for a condition that results in the overproduction of a form of yeast normally found in the body at low levels. In chronic Candidiasis, the rapidly multiplying candida changes form. It morphs into its dangerous fungal state and spreads. The idea is that candida feeds off simple carbohydrates and thrives on yeasty products too. It is therefore recommended (though not yet clinically proven as far as most doctors are concerned) to cut out the following, in order, literally, to starve the yeast in the gut where it takes root: sugar (all types), fruit juice (fruit to be kept to a minimum), yeast products (including virtually all breads), fermented products (namely vinegar and soya sauce), malted products, cured meats, mushrooms, peanuts, walnuts, dairy milk (except yoghurt and cottage cheese) – and so the list goes on. And so I was back to lists.

I found it hard, at first, and I wondered whether I was taking it too far given the greater circumstance. I was unsure as to where the fine line should be drawn between following the directives I had been given to the letter and crossing into a new sort of obsessive behaviour over restricting my choice of food. Was I doing this, really, to ensure a rapid reparation of my gut and thus restore my energy, or was this actually the bait I had anxiously been waiting to bite, the one that gave a legitimate excuse, upon prescription, to adopt the more controlled eating habits with which I felt secure? Either way, I chose the stringent path and gradually, in fact, my headaches started to fade. Slowly, the balloon started to deflate and in a few months I was reaching for my favourite pair of jeans. I started regularly going to the gym, without overdoing it, and my muscles began to show once more. None of this happened overnight: most days I still felt hopeless and so far from making headway to any target. But then, suddenly, I was being told that I looked 'healthy', 'glowing', 'fit' – and those words resonated deep down to touch the chords of self-belief that had gone dull. I began to feel 'good about myself'. For a little while.

The question still remains to know whether my body simply caught up with the times and realised that I had no further intention of starving myself, ever again, or if it was actually because of the anti-candida approach, together with gut-healing supplements and an exercise routine set in place, that I was able to find the figure I recognised to be my natural form. What is important, however, is to note that I was in fact *able* to return to a more comfortable size and that my body would not continue to bulge and bloat against my will.

It is important because that was when, at last, I was able to accept myself, slip back into my resurrected skin and draw connection from an inner strength inside finally to reach out to those surrounding me from the start. Things fell back into place and I was moving forward to a dazzling bright place at a positively upbeat pace. I loved going to the gym. It made me feel so good to be back in myself and exercise brought me that much more in touch with, and connected to, my body. There was always the danger that I would transfer my kitchen drills to the treadmill. But my attitude towards exercise, for now, was not a fixation, not a new-found addiction, nothing menacing. At the gym I was simply able to find my *me*-space, cut off momentarily from any hurly-burly above ground; music on, commotion out. Just for an hour. I was lucky enough to find a trainer at the gym, Penny, who agreed to coach me so that I could learn exactly how to rebuild the muscle I had lost, in an appropriate amount of time and making best use of weights. Penny knew where I was coming from and understood my needs. She helped me become aware of my body; tune into it; realise the wonder of it; have *fun* with it. With her, I took prescribed rest weeks whenever she thought I needed time-out. Alone, I still would not be able to give myself that break. With Penny I began to feel stronger again, both inside and out. My shoulders opened up, now held by a more solid back.

Still, however, no period. In the past, every time I hit a target weight it would come back with exact precision, like a control that needed just enough pressure to be switched on. But this round I had gone far deeper than ever before. My body had emerged from the torment I put it through relatively unsullied, but it couldn't yet tell for sure that I could bear an infant; in any case there remained another child I needed to tend to first, the one whose picture I recognised in photographs of me as a little girl. Still, the point remained that I was without a period – reduced to a pre-pubescent girl's biological form. It had been over a year.

Then, one winter's morning I stumbled from bed to bathroom and there I was greeted with a blotch. Heart-thumps, head-rush, tremble-fingers dialling one phone number after the other announcing the return of 'me'. That was the final signal that everything was now okay, that necessary connections had been made. That I was fully functional and need no longer worry about problems conceiving a child, at least not on the face of things. My period was painful, long and heavy. And I felt heavy too. It was a period of adjustment, one I found harder to handle than my original splurge of joy had foreseen. My period came that month, and another followed the next. Then it went unnoticed, and then I noticed it had gone once more.

So I decided it was time to see a doctor. That was in March 2005. I was now 22 and, aside from that two-month break, I had not had a period for two years.

Smear test, pelvic scan, test tubes, vials of burgundy surging out of my veins. I spent a few weeks waiting and

I turned up in my gynaecologist's office for my results. I already knew there was still some candida in my gut that was causing thrush down below, that was nothing new. I also was aware of another bacterial infection, nothing gruesome, just a consequence of my hormonal imbalance. But then she threw light upon a new snag; all I heard was a stream of -isms, -omes and -ologies. There was no time for questions. I was handed a prescription where she had scribbled a few lines of unintelligible characters and closed with a curvy-swerved signature at the bottom of the page. But this, I was gracefully explained, was only to treat the bacterial irritation; for the rest (what rest? the what did she call it?) there was unfortunately nothing we could do: it was just one of those things to which I would have to grow accustomed. Thank you, goodbye. I followed orders to walk myself downstairs to the basement where I would, conveniently, find a little pharmacy that sold everything I needed. There I met a procession of sweaty patients, losing patience. I lost mine too, stepped outside and found a high-street chemist instead. All this, in one of London's highly reputed hospitals.

Back home I switched on my computer and Googled her professional jargon: Polycystic ovarian disease. Disease was the one scary word I had understood back in that muddy-green gynaecologist's office and it had tap-danced in my mind ever since, giving me, by now, a throbbing headache. What I found made me feel uneasy; all descriptions were forbidding. There was even an association out there in support of women who suffered from my condition.

Polycystic (literally, many cysts) ovary syndrome is a complex condition that affects the ovaries.

In PCOS, the ovaries are bigger than average, and the outer surface of the ovary has an abnormally large number of small follicles (the sac of fluid that grows around the egg under the influence of stimulating hormones from the brain).

In PCOS, these follicles remain immature, never growing to full development or ovulating to produce an egg capable of being fertilised. For the woman this means that she rarely ovulates (releases an egg) and so is less fertile. In addition, she does not have regular periods and may go for many weeks without a period. Other features of the condition are excess weight and excess body hair. Obesity is a common finding in women with PCOS because their body cells are resistant to the sugar-control hormone insulin. This insulin resistance prevents cells using sugar in the blood normally and the sugar is stored as fat instead. (http://www.netdoctor.co.uk/womenshealth/facts/pcos.htm)

Petrified, I turned to Sam, my brother and my sister in turn. If this was as serious as it sounded I was not yet ready to break the news to my parents – because I still needed to protect them, because I didn't want to worry them but, maybe, also because I was afraid of disappointing them. I spent days behind my computer screen, scrolling through page after page of contradictory accounts, until my brain sizzled with information overload. That was not the way to do it. So I summoned courage and plucked out a nerve of bravery to call my dad – the scientist. As always, he took the news with gentle calm and was quick to question the doctor's finding. PCOS is particularly acute in diabetic patients and so happened to be a condition with which he was quite familiar. First of all, it was not a disease. And anyway he found it highly unlikely that I should be suffering from such a syndrome.

I was sent to an expert endocrinologist. All it took was one look at me for him to reject the nerve-racking verdict I held in a shaking hand. What I *did* have, were polycystic ovaries. But not *PCOD*. And it was entirely to be expected at this stage. Effectively, my reproductive system resembled that of a pre-pubescent girl with many follicles waiting to become active but without the fine-tuning of my system yet quite in place to give them the go-ahead. All was in place for a healthy period to come, but my machinery still needed oiling. *Oiling*. I needed to put on weight, just a touch, again. The truth is that, for a while now, I had been wobbling on a see-saw, one foot on either side, carefully keeping balance. I had lost a little too much weight. It wasn't drastic, it just meant that I had no reserves should anything go wrong. The dreaded puffiness had gone, but I had shed one kilo too many after that. More blood was drawn from my right arm and I was given a date to have a bone density assessment too. Those assessments, I wanted so much to believe that there would be no more. And yet, it seemed that they continued to crop up every six months or so, more serious than habitual check-ups. They were the inevitable aftermath of a very serious disorder, which could have physical repercussions in the long run. Not always, but it was important to make sure. I felt tired. Sick of see-saws. Exhausted.

Sam finished law school that year and had six months free before starting as a trainee. Here was his chance to travel and let off steam that, whether he likes to admit to it or not, inevitably boiled up inside of him over our three-some years together: Sam, me and anorexia. He was given an opportunity of work experience in India, for the full duration of his break. And he took it. I gulped; throat tight. This would be a very good thing for me (for him, for *us*). But also dreadfully hard. Sam had been my rock for so long that I had forgotten where to look for strength inside. I had grown so used to having him there, next to me, encouraging and caring for me. Sam cooked nearly every meal for me and it was only with him around that I found the security to leave the house when it went dark outside. Sam was my second half, my *better* half, and I would feel incomplete when he was gone. Sam's presence made me feel calm and reassured. I hated it whenever he chose to 'do his own thing'; I felt hurt if he preferred a boys' night out to a cosy evening at home with me. And yet he spent almost all his evenings at home with me, just the two of us in front of a film. He turned down so many invitations from his friends to party, go clubbing, have some fun, because he knew the scene that it would cause. And on the rare occasions that he did decide to stand up for himself, his resolution was met with furious glares, silence of outrage, then angry, unwarranted arguments and, ultimately, tears. I was ashamed of myself when I reacted that way. I heard the things I said and knew how wrong I was. Yet, inevitably, there was always the same emotional spill, and sometimes he gave in. There was an extended period of transition in which Sam was afraid of upsetting me and acutely aware of how much I had become needy of him. He had seen such ugly things happen not so long ago that he was prepared to sacrifice a large portion of his freedom to make sure I kept every bit of mine. And that was not fair.

I panicked whenever he announced that he was meeting with friends, even when he promised he wouldn't be back home too late. It was like when I was a very little girl and my parents told me they were going out. That made me cry and I would plead desperately for them to stay. As though I was afraid that they would never return. As if their leaving me behind made me feel unloved. I couldn't deal with being around Sam when he was drunk because his utter loss of discipline made me, in turn, feel out of control. That narrowed the opportunities for me to party by his side. I only ever accepted on condition that he promised not to drink too much – and then when we drove back home I would always accuse his eyes of looking hazy, his breath smelling of beer, his voice of sounding slurred. And he would usually retort in a long stream of defence. Come to think of it, things were not going all that well and something had to happen to set us back on track. So India was an opportunity for him to regain independence, for me to learn to rely on myself once more, and for our couple to redeem much necessary individualism from within.

I dreaded his departure and hated the day he had to go. Yet upon saying goodbye I was swept with such romantic melancholy that it felt tender where I imagined it would hurt too much to say. And though I slept very little, the following morning I got up on my feet and already then it was as though I had grown up overnight. I had become blind to the boundaries that separated Sam's personal space from mine. I had lost the capacity to distinguish him as a person apart from me and in so doing I had taken his presence for granted. Now I looked forward to seeing him again and spending time with him, for him. Far from incomplete I felt all the stronger for it. I remembered that I was capable of spending time alone and appreciated the moments I had, just quiet, with myself. I made efforts to see friends and realised I didn't need a chaperone to stay out once the sun had set. When Sam went far away for a very long time I finally dared to step into full-sized shoes. And it was an altogether more poised, level-headed and assertive girlfriend he found upon his return. I threw the cracked mask of neediness away.

21

The day of my bone density scan came. I had never had one of these before, though I had been advised to do so even in my early Geneva days, because back then it felt like one more heavy interference piling on to too many hospital, medical, clinical, pharmaceutical interventions all at once. But now it was necessary because I had been without a period for too long, menopausal in effect, and that hormonal imbalance was bound to impact negatively on my skeletal mass.

It was not a scary procedure having this Star Trek-like machine zooming over you as you lay very still. But I was smacked with a stark reality check when given my results. Here is a copy of the letter that was sent to my GP:

30 August 2006 (aged 23)

Emily's BMD is giving me some cause for concern – she has frank osteoporosis in the spine and reduced density in the femur.

Bam.

The letter came when Sam was away and I was by myself in London. I felt alone.

I felt afraid. I cried. I went to see Vicki, whom I hadn't seen for a while, and we discussed the pros and cons of Hormonal Replacement Therapy, to which I was vehemently opposed. She suggested we try to tackle the thing by natural means. The *thing*. It was all so surreal and the truth of it had not yet fully hit me. I think I was more frightened by the sound of the words than I was aware of their meaning. What I needed though, urgently now, was for my period to return. Hormones might make that happen, but what would happen were I to choose to stop taking those little pills one day? And what of all the articles I had read that linked HRT to breast cancer amongst others? It was, of course, a matter of weighing the lesser of two evil eventualities, but still. I wanted to sort this out myself without any chemical assistance. I needed a little bit of time – and it was reluctantly granted to me by my doctor with a view to re-assessing the situation in three months' time. I felt that I could do this. It was the final push. But then the immediate fear factor wore off and the sense of emergency faded away. All that fuss was shoved in my to-be-filed drawer, the messy one I somehow never find the time to sort through.

Louise and I had agreed that after two years it might be best for me to see somebody else, someone who would offer a fresh perspective with, perhaps, a different approach more suited to my current needs. I had the image of a box that Louise had helped me build, and now I needed somebody else to help me fill it with useful tools – and teach me how to use them too. Tools with which to handle little ordeals of my everyday life and, ultimately, to manage the bigger hurdles that would inevitably be thrown at me once in a while. I had looked, briefly, for a cognitive behavioural therapist. This was a method about which I had heard great things and I believed it best adapted to the state of mind I had now reached: logical, practical thinking. But I didn't find anyone that clicked. And the truth is that I didn't actually look all that far. Because while I saw that I still needed a little more psychological support to stabilise the progress I had made so far and I was willing, to a degree, to accept that I now had to regain a couple of kilos for my period to kick back into gear, still I felt that I was also way out of any real danger of slipping back and wanted to do this on my own. Recovery is such a tricky stage to define, and often so much more draining than staying stuck in the mess of that ugly disease. It is difficult to decide when the time has come to 'move on' and 'take it easy'; when to let go of the therapy, the weekly sessions, the deep-and-meaningfuls, the 'how are you feeling and what will you take away with you today'. Does that time ever come? It's fine, stop the official analysis, but no, don't *ever* end your treatment of yourself.

For a year I had been working on a project with a friend, building a web-based company with the aim of facilitating – and improving, perhaps – meal-time decision-making for parents with young children. The service was to provide weekly personalised meal-planners, complete with recipes, serving suggestions, cooking tips, shopping lists and essential nutritional guidelines – all approved by a team of professional nutritionists, taking into account the child's dietary needs, physical activity, potential allergies, as well as the parents' budget and cooking capabilities. Far from being ironic, this was me trying to turn my experience around and to make the most of all that I had learned, through reading and with Vicki, about nutrition, healthy diets and restoring colour to a meal for it to be tempting with all things good. In brief, it was a grand enterprise and one to which I dedicated all my time, all my heart, and all the rest of me too. There was no more time for therapy, no need because I was out of the crisis-zone and it was all beginning to sound like psycho-babble when I had more important things to do. So I began to amble alone, with my head buried deep under a swarm of tasks. I should have paced myself. But the trouble is I never really learned how. I am not one for half measures, and this applies even to the way I feel about people or react to most situations. There is little room for shades in the colour spectrum of my world. I had taken my anorexia to its extreme. Likewise I then pushed the accelerator on my resurgence from hell faster than either Vicki or Louise would ever have thought could be true. It was spectacular and they were astonished. From perfect anorexic I shifted into perfect anorexic in recovery; but the problem is that I never let go of perfection.

We launched our company in November 2006. It was exciting at first and felt so rewarding to see all our intensive hard labour come to fruition at last. But trying to get a company off the ground; having to sell yourself and deal with occasional negative response; managing glitches and overcoming setbacks; running a company day-in-day-out where home becomes office and work-leisure boundaries become completely blurred – all these things require:

1. *determination* – which I had
2. *willpower* – which I had
3. *resolve* – which I had

4. *drive* – which I had
5. *self-control* – of which I had too much
6. *self-discipline* – of which I had too much
7. *the capacity to handle disappointment* – which I lacked
8. *the capacity to cope with things not always working out to plan* – which I lacked, utterly
9. *the capacity not to feel a failure (and all associated negative feelings) should the project not take off* – which I lacked, utterly
10. *the capacity to keep perspective, at all times* – a word so alien to me that it still sounds foreign today

And it was these last few that caused me to trip. Because things didn't happen the way they were supposed to and we had constantly to rethink, reconsider, reassess. That's all part of the game, all part of being an entrepreneur – a good sign that we were acting professionally in fact. But the trouble is that it began to cause me to reassess myself, because I wasn't capable of compartmentalising, of drawing much-needed lines; to distinguish between evaluating the success of this venture and valuing my own sense of achievement. Achievement. That need to feel significant; that fear of letting everyone down, my parents, my friends, anyone who ever stored the slightest amount of faith in me: I owed it to live up to all their expectations. Compliments were not flattering: they went straight to the stockpile of pressure. And yet who was I letting down, in fact? Who was applying pressure on me, more and more, all the time? Who expected so much out of me, too much? I needed desperately to learn to love myself. I was still my only real opponent; my greatest rival was myself. It had always been me that was hurting me.

22

The truth is that from the moment I stepped out of the immediate emergency situation, I inadvertently put my recovery on pause, or perhaps I even pressed the 'stop' button by mistake. Either way, I thought that since I was ostensibly feeling okay, and my life seemed to have fallen right back into its proper place, it was unnecessary for me to continue spending so much time (and money) on myself. I was fine, and that was how I was going to behave: fine. What I realise now is that, actually, I still hated to look at my body in a mirror and preferred for lights to be dimmed when I was getting undressed. And I still wanted to keep a T-shirt on even in my most intimate moments (which had in fact hugely improved) with Sam. I still had a warped sense of self-worth which still could only be measured against everyone else's appreciation (or not) of me and I still tended to think of anyone who met me for the very first time that they really, *really*, did not like me at all. And, occasionally, I found it hard to go out at night and, sometimes, restaurant choice became more of an issue again – not always, but often enough for me to notice, silently. I never arrived at a point, really, where I could eat everything I would have once happily enjoyed and essentially always ended up having 'my own thing' even when invited over for dinner. Fundamentally, I never actually gave myself a break, and as a result I never came to appreciate, let alone love, the person that I was; the person that I am.

If I walked away from recovery it was because I wanted so much for everyone to be pleased about how much progress I had made and how far I had come. I wanted my parents, my family, my Sam, my therapists and friends, I wanted them all to smile at the thought of me and rest assured that I was doing swimmingly well, paddling happily along, nothing to worry about any more. I never gave Louise, nor anyone else, the chance to take me just a little further, to a place where any of life's unavoidable emotional shudders would not inevitably wobble me physically out of place.

Then the thunder struck. Another unexpected phone call; I have come to fear that ring. Sam, from India. His voice trembling; muffled. His language sounded foreign and I could not grasp his words. He repeated himself. This time I heard.

'*It has spread to her lungs; she has days.*' Sue. Sam's mum. Days.

The numbness, the shivers, the cold; all a familiar fore-cast of feelings I thought had been dissolved. Where are the covers? Where is the blanket? Where is the warmth of a hug in which I want to hide?

I remember the weeks that followed like the one scene that marks you in a film. Except this was reality. And reality hit hard.

Sam was on a plane coming home. I waited for him at the airport. His return. That Hollywood moment long awaited where I would rush to give him a languid kiss and he would hold me up and he would twirl me around and we would laugh. Sliding doors. There he was. And I ran to him, just like I always would. And he held me, tight, so very tight, in his arms, just like he always did. Except the script had changed. My opening line was no longer 'I love you and am so happy you are back'. Instead I said, 'She is okay. We are driving straight to the hospital. She is still there. She has not gone.'

We held on strongly to her hands and gathered strength from the calm in Sam's mother's eyes. So serene, peaceful and composed. So much light around this angel while the situation was so terrifyingly dark. Neon. Clinical stench. The food they offered in hospital all dreary shades of brown, brownish-orange, brownish-green, brownish-yellow. She would not eat that food. Every day from home a hamper filled with treats travelled 'the fast route' to her bed. Apple stews, soups, purées, soya yoghurt, softened oats. Nothing too chewy. Nothing too hard. Things that were easy to digest. I had sent her a 'happy pack' from London before we arrived: 'Little Miss Happy', 'The Tao of Pooh', cosy soft pink socks, and her favourite granola bars, crunchy honey-seed squares, the organic chocolate she always nibbled at home with naughty delight, one or two squares more than what she originally laid out on her plate, then neatly wrapped up and back into its drawer where Sam would scurry for a midnight treat. One evening I went to the larder to find a tin of corn. There were the bars, the squares, the chocolate untouched. They were all too chewy, too hard, too difficult to digest. I didn't know. I felt guilty. Upset. I hadn't got it right. *Not good enough*. Regardless of the intention. Stupid me.

Days went by. Each a blessed gift. One more day. One more day. And then no more. By her side was Sam, his brother Ben and Peter, his dad, talking to her all through the night. And we, Ben's fiancée and I, taking turns at sitting behind the boys, resting what solace we could on their shoulders. Promises were made in whispers to her ear that we would all be there for each other. That she could fly away gracefully in the peace that she had spread.

Numb. Shivering. Cold. Surreal.

There were tears, and laughter. There were smiles shining what brightness they could through looks of despair. Sadness, sorrow; aching, throbbing pain. There are no words that really can tell. It hurt because it hurt. It hurt because they hurt. It hurt to see them hurt. It stung. The sting.

I needed to be strong. It was my turn to be the crutch, my turn to be there for Sam. And yet I felt so weak. My legs were shaking; I could barely hold myself up.

I must be strong. I feel so frail. I must be strong.

The autumn leaves were so vivid that year; it seemed that nature was mourning too, but with dazzling colours of hope.

I must be strong. I feel afraid. So deeply, deeply afraid.

23

I was not strong enough.

I realise now how important it is to put some time aside, *every* day, to do something special, for yourself. Every day to take a moment to check in on yourself and deal with whatever might be churning inside, on the spot, before it curdles. And sometimes, maybe even more often than not, there may in fact be nothing wrong. Still, on those days above all, it is so essential really to make the most of our happiness. It all may sound a little tacky and may be read as sickly-sweet twaddle, indeed that is exactly how I would have reacted in the past. Why do we find it so hard to listen to anything remotely spiritual or to do with taking care of one's self without disappearing behind a cynical snigger?

I am seeing Vicki and Louise again. To get me back on track. I am going to take my healing into recovery and I am going to put some tools in that toolbox of mine. I wrote this letter to my parents, to Patrick and to Sam the other day:

13 June 2007 (aged 24)

*So I saw Louise last night and I was SO relieved to go back
to see her. She said at first that she was sad that I had
slipped, because I was her little star patient who bounced so
far forward from so far back when both Vicki and she
never thought they would manage to get me better. But she
also said that she was glad because I was there and that was
the key to any recovery. She said that people do slip in
recovery and that I was not the person she met for the first
time three years ago (that long!) She did not in fact say
that she 'saw it coming' quite as explicitly as that, but that
from the moment I was 'okay' she saw this obsessive
behaviour, taking no holiday, burying my head into
accomplishing this project and putting myself second. She
said that so often, just because the 'crisis' is over, people
forget themselves and everything comes first. And I recognise
myself there.*

*She wasn't all 'psychobabble' as you may cynically say,
and she wasn't suggesting that I should be in therapy for the
rest of my life, but that I never really pushed my therapy as
far as I should have done in order to be fully equipped with
tools to prevent this kind of a slip from happening in the*

future. I need to underline that none of this was said in a Dr D-like 'I told you so' vengeful manner, but rather simply giving me her point of view, listening to where I have been in the past nine months and letting me know that she was happy (while sad) to see me because she cares enormously about me.

We then discussed my coming back to see her. I said that I had seen three other therapists and none had clicked. She knew the last woman actually and saw why that didn't work. I asked if she would be willing to see me again and whether she thought it was a good idea. I explained how comfortable I felt with her and that she got me in ways no one else did and that while at the time I thought I needed something else, the truth is that I never let her push me, really, because I wasn't ready to look a little deeper at things and that, effectively, I have been doing intensive therapy through writing for the past four months and it has brought me to so much more mature a place in terms of being disposed to making the most of my time with her now. She said she would, and that it was ultimately all about what worked best for me. She did say that if we were going to work together she wanted a commitment from me, that my well-being was to come first, before anything else, and that if she suggests a workshop or another activity that she thinks can only help, that I trust she is doing so because she believes it is right and that whereas before there were *financial excuses or other back-out clauses, she now wants a promise that while I don't have to stick everything through, still that I will give things a go.*

I talked to her about going to a group thing and she said she was going to suggest that herself. She, like me, doesn't think I should go to a food group because she thinks I am more of an 'overall' person and that the food groups might drag me down into the disease rather than help me out of it. But there are so many groups out there, and ultimately all addictions are basically the same. Being in a group means you benefit from hearing other people's stories, and about their shit days too and you get so much more feedback on your own stuff, while professionally monitored. All this meaning that you gain perspective on things and learn to let go – both of which I desperately need.

She said she is going to think about different groups that exist and ask around to find the one she feels is best suited for me. She will call me before the end of the week with those details and meanwhile work out a plan of action for me, and call Vicki so that they are both working together once again.

All this to say that I am back on track in terms of a real support network that I trust and trust will turn this thing around before it gets out of hand.

Sam is coming to Vicki's with me tonight because he wants to ask her about food given that he cooks basically every night, and he wants her to give him recipe ideas with which I will be happy etc ... I am a very lucky girl to have him in my life but I am also treading dangerous ground because he is exhausted and all this is very tough on him. He said last night that he was so happy that finally after months of looking for people and the right people falling pregnant (I had found a wonderful GP but she announced soon after that she was going on maternity leave for six months) or not being around (Vicki was abroad for several months too) we have secured a safety net once more. But he also said that just like when he catches a smell that reminds him of the flat in Oxford or sees a photo of me back then it makes him sick to the stomach, likewise hearing me mention Vicki and Louise brings back horrifying memories. So, while I am getting myself back in order for you – and Patrick – I also really need to do this for him. It has been hard for him and while we never really talked about it, he has been trying to be both supportive and also giving me the same warning signals as you have for just as long if not longer.

I did tell him though that this was not me broken. This was me going in for servicing because the flashing light has turned on. It's like I could drive all the way to Oxford and back but I am risking breaking down on the motorway at any time if I don't service the car right now, before it breaks down. And that is exactly what this is. The final push we

*have all been talking about for the past few months or so
but never managed to find the right people to help me walk
it. Now I have.*

And then I wrote this second letter to my brother a few
days later:

Only good news this week. I feel so hopeful.

*I saw Vicki yesterday and she was actually, you will be
pleased to hear, firmer than ever before. She said we were
going to turn this thing around fast and that she was going
to push me this time, because I am strong enough now to
handle it, and set weekly challenges which I may not always
find easy to meet but which I will, because I have to trust her
(and I do, which is why this is going to work). I voiced my
fears of bloating out and the puffiness, headaches, lethargy I
suffered from back at the time. She said the good news was
that I had been through that already and that we had
together established what food groups triggered such reactions,
what foods did not (or no longer) agree with me, and that we
were going to work with those that did while extending the
range of variety within that category of 'tolerated' ingredients.*

*For the moment, it is about getting me to let go. And for
that I need to step out of my comfort zone ever so slowly. If I
need to stick to safe foods once in a while that's fine, but it will
be with her guidelines of quantities in mind. We are meeting*

Perfect

at WholeFoods on Friday to do a supermarket checklist together
so we can actually walk around the shop and look at specific
products and comment on them. This way she can gauge my
reaction to, and interaction with, food as well. That way also
I am not just walking away from her office with a long list
which I could then just discard out of laziness when shopping
under the pretext that I can't find the stuff or whatever. So we
are meeting at 4 p.m., notepad in hand, for checklists and
recipe ideas. And we are going to do the same with Sainsbury's
and Tesco so that I have the flexibility not to have to stick to
WF or starve (you know what I mean) because I can't find the
exact product I want elsewhere. I can't wait! Because she is so
dynamic and colourful and enthusiastic it can only be an
inspiring experience.

Sam came for the last 20 minutes and she told him that
for now he also needed to let go. He has enough on his plate
to worry about and I am now in good hands. For now, she
said she needed him to trust that she knew exactly what
she was doing and that we could carry on eating together
and enjoying our meals but that it would still have to be
me doing my thing and him doing his, or us doing the same
and his adding whatever oil, pesto or anything else he
wanted to his plate. She underlined that it was not his job
to take care of me and that it was not healthy for either of
us nor our relationship for him to feel such responsibility.
She told him she knew the feeling of frustration when you

want to rip your hair out because you just wish the person in front of you, whom you love, could pick up a spoon and gobble a bucket-full of ice cream. But, she reiterated, he needs to let go and while she was sensitive enough to tell him he was still a really important part of this and that he needn't just buzz off to the sidelines and hide in a corner, it was just about trusting her — and me.

So there!

Vicki is great because she knows me inside out (literally) and above all I trust her so much that I will tell her the complete total and utter truth because I know she will never criticise, judge or belittle me.

And the immediate replies I received make me realise, once more, how lucky I am to be surrounded by so much immeasurable love, boundless.

From my father

Bottom line: as Louise says, you are your priority right now.

Love you (to be read in both its senses — as an order and a daddy statement of fact).

From my brother

Twirp — what can I say except that I am really, really happy. My frustration over the last few months has been only your inaction and now something is happening and that is all I wanted.

I think one of your biggest fears is disappointing others. You really have to learn to look at your decisions through your own eyes and be your own judge of whether you are comfortable with things or not. I know that we have all put you on a pedestal for so long and that it is so scary to be on that pedestal because you feel everybody has such high expectations. We keep telling you that you are special, beautiful, smart and can't do anything wrong and it is precisely this that is very hard to deal with. The main thing you have to do is not care about all this and actually learn to do things that make you happy even if they won't necessarily make others happy. A healthy dose of apathy is not necessarily such a bad thing (trust me!) What you have to learn is that we actually love you enough that you can disappoint us and it won't matter.

Your annoying big brother who loves you.

From my mother

Bravo for all these positive steps forward and for having taken stock and recognised the urgency of the situation. It is always so much easier to hide behind excuses or to bury our heads in denial. This is not your case, and that requires courage.

I am so proud of the manner in which you took the initiative to steer your way back on to your recovery tracks. We are all here, just as we always have been and always will, to back you up and support you with love and faith. You will get there fast.

I love you.

From Sam, such words of encouragement came frequently to remind me of his constant support:

You probably don't need me to say this again, but I will, that what is more important than anything is getting you to a healthy weight and happy place. You do need to take this seriously and see the right people in London, and not put it off. This is the new leaf and the final push, so do something every day that scares you a little.

I love you x

Conclusion

erfect is the book I set out to write. But the book that I wrote is not perfect. Because *I* am not perfect. And nor will I ever be. I know that now. And I now know that's okay.

There are four questions that always arise whenever I make mention of anorexia in my life: *why* did it happen; *how* did it come about; *what* marked a turning point in my recovery and *whether* I think it can ever go 'for good'.

My aim was originally to compose a detailed essay that would seek to answer these questions, systematically, in turn. I hoped for things to become more clear by the end of it; I intended to analyse, rationalise, box my story up and wrap it with a neat string of perfect common sense. How anorexic of me.

I have come to the closing chapter of my book, and still I cannot say why, nor how, nor what, whether or when. And those are the uncertainties with which I must learn to live – amongst the many other doubts, ambiguities and unknowns that I – that we – must come simply to accept, humbly.

At several points in my life, for various reasons, I began to feel insecure and *afraid*. My reasons are immaterial, as would be yours, because it is the *feelings* they caused that can universally be shared. These feelings, progressively unspoken over time, grew to take unprecedented dimensions and to bundle themselves up into a tangled, knotty lump at the pit of my stomach.

And as that lump swelled and spread, so I looked, unwittingly, somehow for ways in which to cover up the fear and smother it with a thick layer of seemingly flawless control: to be the best at what little there was left for me to monitor. To be perfect as a daughter, sister, friend, student, customer, as a person, became my goal. The more I found to regulate, the thicker that padding of control, in perfection, and so the safer, more secure, I (thought I) felt.

It so followed that the natural progression of my newfound shield from harm would be to master *hunger* – the most basic, fundamental sensation of need shared by all. If our very existence is ultimately sustained through nourishment, then to exercise unwavering, unshakable control over food, surely, was to be in total, utter, powerful control over *life*.

To be the perfect anorexic then turned out my golden key to acquiring supreme defence against all anguish.

Anorexia would crush my fear. Or so I believed at the time. But anorexia is a liar; and she turns your life into a lie. She is destructive, perverse, devious, cunning, scheming, and evil. Anorexia cures no pain. Anorexia *is* a pain. And anorexia is painful.

I hope that in and amongst these lines I will have conveyed as real an experience as language can ever express and that whoever should read my words will draw from them the torture that is this disease. And may it be drawn clearly that it is, in fact, a disease; not a fad, not an aspiration, not a game nor any passing phase. Not anyone's *fault*.

Cruella came; she grew, she shrank, she stung, she fizzled out; she conquered, she lost, she prevailed then she went under. She is a veritable demon, always threatening to infect my blood once more. And I must always take care not to let that happen again. I must always take care of myself.

I was lucky. And I am grateful. From the moment my anorexia was defined I never denied it. I looked for help, listened to help; let help in. This, I was told, would save me. I was open and willing to talk about my condition. I wanted to in fact; so people would understand and forgive me for not being myself – it meant that I could begin to forgive myself too. It meant, also, that I never became alien to my friends; and my friends never let me go. I don't know where I would be today without them.

I was lucky to be surrounded, always, by a family that bore no judgement and continued to trust in my ability to heal. My parents offered me support without compromise, flagged by endless words of encouragement. They never ceased to believe in me and that fuelled what little confidence I had left inside. They gave me so much; they were my crutch, my safety net, my raft. All they ever wanted was to see me grow, and glow. I owed it to them to find that light.

My siblings never made me feel guilty for all the attention that was inevitably focused my way. They stood up for me, and by my side, whenever they could. My family kept faith in me; and I kept faith because of them – I could not let them down.

I was fortunate to meet Vicki and Louise who, together, helped me to help myself. Once again, key to the success of their methods was the fact that they never judged; they did not punish and never belittled me with the sense of failure. They took away my whip and convinced me that I deserved to give myself a break; that it was time to breathe in with the good and out with the bad. Together, they taught me trust; to trust myself, to trust in others, to trust in food too.

And then there was Sam. Sam who stroked my heart to a peaceful beat. He was always able, somehow, to distinguish between Cruella and me – and he never admitted defeat. His eyes: the softness of them, the way he looked at me, straight through to the girl he had chosen to love; they held me up and spurred me upwards. I am lucky.

I want to say thank you. Again and again. *Thank you.*

There is no perfect conclusion to be written; I am not sure there is any real conclusion at all. But I think there are ways to keep our heads above water. And there are a few important messages with which I want to close.

I want to underline how important it is to reach out for help – I want to say reach out *to* help.

Never give up hope.

I want to shout out loud that love does not depend on 'perfection'. And that the greatest proof of love is to let yourself *be* loved. But, to let love in, to let it spread, you have to start with learning to accept who you are, and to love that person too, in all your blemishes and flaws.

I want to remind – and remember – that life isn't always easy; sometimes it *will* all feel 'too much'. But that *this too will pass.* Really, it does.

I want to say *let go.* To you; to me, too. Anorexia is about being afraid of being afraid. We all are afraid, some more – and sometimes more – than others. It is how we *deal* with that fear – whether we deal with it at all – that differs from person to person. Whether we be worried about growing up, dreading what comes next, or frightened because we do not know what the future has in store; whether it be anguish at the thought of not 'achieving' something, 'becoming' someone, living a life in 'accomplishment'. Any repressed emotion is generally contained in fear – the fear of *feeling*. Ultimately, so many of us are just afraid of being afraid. Anorexia seeks to stifle that fear; and as a result, held back, it grows.

So feel your fear, face your fear, embrace your fear, because behind uncertainty there lies a million exciting possibilities. Fear is your adventure, and mine.

Perfection is a trick; it is an elusive artifice of the mind. Perfection is the bar that keeps rising. It is a rope knotted tightly at the throat; a suffocating ideal that holds you back with a choke. Anorexia seduced me with her promises of perfection. She made me believe I could achieve the unachievable; obtain the unobtainable. Today I know that I can't. Today I want to believe in *me*, in my capacity to live without anorexia; in my ability to free myself of perfection. I want to live.

How does it end? It doesn't. This is the beginning.

Afterword

I wanted to dedicate this chapter to those who suffered my anorexia in silence, by my side, in her shadow. I wanted this to be an opportunity for them to express the way they felt, the way they feel. I wanted them to be able to say how Cruella hurt them too. I also thought that this would be a way to help other such voiceless victims find solace; for parents to hear that they are not alone in feeling utterly helpless and riddled with an anguish that few words can express; for siblings to know that it is okay to feel angry at times, exasperated, outraged even. I wanted Sam and Olivia, as boyfriend and best friend, to reach out to others by tapping into their experience of 'the horror' too.

I asked my family, Olivia and Sam to write without giving them too many guidelines. I wanted it to be spontaneous, and to come from somewhere deep inside, somewhere real, and raw. I only said that the idea was for them to say how they first reacted on hearing the (dreaded) word 'anorexia' tagged to their daughter, sister, friend, lover. And then to talk about how they lived through and dealt with 'second-hand anorexia'. I asked them not to hold back, not to tread on eggshells, not to worry about how I might receive their words. I was ready to hear what they had to say. I wanted them to tell me, and to tell you.

This proved a more arduous task than I had anticipated, for some more than for others, and I am no longer sure that the premise of this chapter remains the same. It's not easy for everyone to put pen to paper, I realise that now. My sister, I know, found it particularly hard to talk about her feelings, firstly because it is not like her to lay them out in public, but also because I have kept her at a distance in recent years: sisterhood is a complicated thing. I assumed that my loved ones would want to look back, that it could only be cathartic for them to remember. I took it for granted that, like me, everyone feels comfortable in the written word and that unthinkable truths transpire in writing. But sometimes people want to move on. It is time for us to move on.

So I hand my pages over to the voices of those who offered support that I will never forget and fuelled me with a love that was, that is, larger than life itself. And even if the end result is not what it set out to be, still I keep my fingers crossed that these words will echo unspoken impressions of those who do not have a chance to voice their own; that others may find comfort in, and empathise with them – and that this may be a chance for more communication to follow.

From Maman to mothers:

I remember saying, with such certainty, the fatal phrase: 'if there is one person who moves through life light as air and without any worries, who is always happy; if there is one person who will never run the risk of becoming anorexic, it is Emily'. I was speaking with my mother-in-law at the time, and Emily was about thirteen. Nothing could prove me wrong: I was so certain. And yet.

It all started slowly, slyly, insidiously, until that unforgettable day when Emily came home from school in tears. 'I have lost too much weight and they are no longer sure whether I can be the bride in the fashion show.' I tried to comfort her by minimising the importance of the event, telling her (convincing myself) this was just a passing phase, that she was simply under more stress than usual. I thought to myself that this was a simple adolescent identity crisis and in reassuring her so I reassured myself.

Shortly after, however, the terrible verdict fell on me, like a time-bomb exploding in revenge for my earlier self-confidence. 'Your daughter is suffering from anorexia.' There was no warning – this came out of a sky that was too blue striking a perfect family, our perfect family; too perfect.

From then on, everything is blurred. I am in denial but the illness is taking root, flouting my arrogance and naïve belief that Emily is immune: my daughter cannot be sick: not with this disease. This is not happening. I cannot bring myself to use the word 'anorexia', I do not want anyone to touch my perfect daughter, I will not let anyone hurt her, I cannot imagine her all alone in a sterile room, stuffed callously like a goose; intimidated, threatened, punished, for what? I don't want to be replaced by a hospital environment without tenderness and affection. No hospital can replace my maternal love; for her to be held from the tenderness, the warmth that a mother can bring. I will not let it happen. Too many imperatives; not enough letting go. I must let go.

Fear stirs aggression in me, and on occasion I am too harsh. I immediately regret my outbursts in the face of her disarming fragility and take her in my arms. Yet I hardly dare touch her any more, I am so frightened of hurting her; her hands are freezing, she is so skinny and her large blue eyes cry out her suffering. I suffer with her and I am scared – she is slipping out of my hands; I am losing her.

I seek desperately for a reason, an explanation. Was I too protective in reaction to my own affective insecurity? Did I trouble my highly sensitive little girl by letting her get too close to my own episode of paralysing anxiety after the two other children left home? Did I disturb her quiet sensitivity with an episode too painful for words to tell when I was once struck with paralysing panic attacks of which she was a silent witness, too close and all alone? Was my anxiety in fact a premonition of what was then still dormant, but looming, in Emily or did it, perhaps, contribute to her latent instability?

Only questions; no answers. Regardless. I feel guilty.

Guilty; guilty of protecting her, of stifling her perhaps, of loving her too much. Guilty of my arrogance, of my maternal presumption, and the overbearing sense of strength in the face of any danger that might seek to strike one of my children. I am guilty of believing that I alone could save her, I who know her better than anyone else, I who fed her from the moment she was born, mother of nourishment cut from her very *raison d'être*.

Yet I am helpless. Utterly helpless.

In spite of herself, Emily is manipulating our emotions. She dominates our family life, I focus all my attention on her and I begin to neglect the rest, starting with Philippe, my husband, our rock, whose strength we tend to overestimate. We load all our worries on to his shoulders. He who puts our happiness and well-being before his own. And then there is Amanda, my other daughter, who so deserved my fullest attention on the most important day of her life, her wedding. And yet I was elsewhere. I am tormented by the deepest regret. Towards Patrick, my son,

I feel no guilt – only gratitude for his continual support, of me, of Emily, of us all.

From time to time, the sun shines through the clouds providing brief respite. Hope is reborn with a smile, one hundred grams gained that transport us with delight; disproportionate delight. Our reflections are deformed. Yet these brief moments of optimism only throw me into even deeper despair when in turn I am again confronted with the crude reality of the situation. Nightmares and visions of horror wake me up in the middle of the night; I am exhausted, I feel wiped out. I am desperate. My impulsive nature, impatient, hurried, always on-the-go, calls eagerly for a quick solution. Yet we seem to be moving forward so slowly, too slowly; what a cruel lesson of fortitude.

We try everything: encouragement, warning, blackmail, promises, charlatans, parallel medicine, clinical treatment. I am at a loss for what to do: I feel lost. Should we protect her or let her go, deliver her to herself? But when do we know if she is master of herself? How do we discern between the daughter we love and the demonic disease that we loathe? When I try to accommodate her I feel that I have become her devil's accomplice. Yet I want to offer support, reassurance; for her to trust me, us, and for her to learn to believe in herself once more. I am in disarray. We try, in desperation, a weekend workshop in London, a descent into the chambers of torture; what is my disembodied angel doing in the midst of such distress? How will the suffering of others help her overcome her own torment? Hell has landed on earth.

We have yet to conquer the final hurdles. They are small, and now feel so surmountable. I am still scared. But we move forward with optimism, faith and trust. All the love that surrounds her, and with the ultimate support of her own enormous (unbelievable) inner strength, we hope to (we *will*) uproot this evil that will have had the merit, despite all the unutterable pain it caused, to teach us to be more tolerant, patient, and humble. Cruella made us accept that it is okay to crash, it is okay to break down and stall; 'she' forced us to let go, to accept, be less cynical, to question ourselves, and above all to recognise that *perfect* is not perfect. It never was.

Thank you, Emily, for all that we have learned. And forgive me, please, for having covered you with so much, too much, adoring protection.

Emily asked me what 'guidance' I could offer to mothers who might be suffering a similar plight …

If I am to retrace the painful experience this journey has been, if I could help, in any way, other mothers who are brought to pass through the tunnel of horror that is this disease, I would tell them never to cut off the lines of communication with your child. To respond and to react quickly, short-circuiting the phase of denial. To find the strength to pull your head out of the sand and face anorexia with resilience; with a determination to fight with the disease, but never with your child. Try to remember that distinction at all times. Always be present – but never over-powering; never judgemental. Never to force, always to try. And to accept; accept disappointment, accept that others may in fact know better, just this once. Accept that these things take time, but to trust; to encourage. And to have patience; so much patience. To be confident, to be atten-tive and offer all the care and support that only a mother can give, but without ignoring other family members in consequence. To face this great challenge without ever giving in to your own fear; but to accept that fear too. And never give up: always have faith in the healing power of *love*.

From Daddy to fathers:

I am the father. I am not a spiritual person but I am more sensitive than my falsely cynical carapace reveals. The irony is that Emily's anorexia may have made me a more caring and affectionate parent, a better person, but the cost, the suffering, is unacceptable. Writing this chapter is hard: I am quite unused to discussing my emotions and wonder how well this will work. It will be important to get the balance right, describing what anorexia can do, has done to my family, without allowing it to dictate its terms even in this exercise, manipulating my words from a distance to throw us all into turmoil (again and again).

Anorexia lives, a pathogen that has invaded the family, all of us, in the most brazen or obscure way, metamorphosing and manipulative, always destructive. A horror. Let me try to explain what it feels like to see my daughter taken over by this terrible force.

A friend, a doctor, told me at the outset that this disease is all about 'self-confidence, self-confidence, self-confidence'. It is, of course, also about control. And guilt: personal, collective and always misplaced guilt.

Anorexia came to us, as probably to any family, in several phases. I am going to try to describe them in chronological order although they obviously overlap and in some cases recur out of order, surprising you from the dark, snatching away whatever comfort one may have found.

The first phase is denial. Emily had lost weight in her last year at school. Slowly at first, hardly perceptible and then a sudden, dramatic loss with obvious changes to her appearance and behaviour. Her friends had picked up on this and some had alerted her and us to her 'situation', not yet a 'condition'. In reality, the phase of denial is of necessity short. Of course Emily's mother and I discussed what was going on right from the start, and maybe denial is not the right word. One simply hopes it will go away. It's the stress of exams; she is frightened of leaving home; that year at the local Swiss school was such a mistake but she'll get over it: she has a great group of friends now; there is no reason for this so it is probably a mistake: we are over-reacting; we never had to go through adolescent rebellion with Emily (always the 'perfect' child ...) and this too will pass, quickly, without consequence.

In all honesty, I am in perpetual denial about something or other, important or trivial. I tuck my head in like a tortoise and wait for the problem to go away. I quite understand how exasperating this is to the family and later, much later, Emily would explain how important it was to show my emotions: better to shout and scream than to be silent. But this was a problem that was not going away and I never learned that particular lesson.

The issue of control is central to the story. Although as I write my chapter I have not read Emily's book, she has surely made this an important part of her story. It is so poignant that the only control she could exercise over her life was depriving herself of food and in essence life. Ironically, as Cruella took over Emily's life, and controlled her, my own control over my immediate (family) surroundings was deformed and ultimately destroyed. Now I was confronted for the first time by a situation that had spun out of control, out of my control certainly, within such a short space of time, just a few months. The denial was over and the situation was very certainly a condition about which I could no nothing.

It is mortifying to have to sit back and watch this horrifying transformation. Emily was a happy child – not superficially so, but a genuinely happy, bright, sparkling, amusing and totally captivating person. Anorexia was totally unexpected. Take it from me: even if you can put it all together neatly after reading the book, we had no clues or hint of what was happening. And when it hits, you lose control. The truth is that there was simply nothing I could do but watch. Of course we spoke, for hours, every day, with Emily. Of course we tried, everything. Anger, reason, bribery, tears and finally desperation. But fundamentally, we had lost the battle before we even knew the enemy.

So we were lost. Completely lost and devastated. Rosane and I were so lucky to find comfort in each other, and Amanda and Patrick played such an important role in helping us as well as Emily. Later there was Sam. The family unit works! Yet even this could have gone wrong. I can well imagine a couple breaking under the stress. How easy it would be, having lost control, to blame it all on the other. How easy for Amanda and Patrick, had they been less exceptional, to be jealous of our irrational obsession with all that was Emily. The stress of anorexia takes you to that breaking point beyond any other. This is a vicious disease that extends far beyond the infected (I use that clinically incorrect word intentionally) person and I too was totally transformed. Not physically but morally. I really did find myself 'lost *with* the enemy'. Anorexia simply takes over like any effective parasite and becomes an all-consuming preoccupation. There is nothing symbiotic about this relationship. It is entirely one-sided. Anorexia drains and destroys.

You cannot imagine what happens. Soon, we were all living with anorexia. The impact is quite extraordinary. Emily will have described her own suffering and that is of course at the heart of this darkness. The parents are silent witnesses. Not literally, but virtually. The horror is indescribable. This sweet, sweet pea is killing herself in front of you. The little girl has become a monster. I do not mean this as it sounds; it was on occasion simply hard to take that deep breath and remember that this was Cruella not Emily. Nobody in the family suffered as much as Emily, but we did all suffer. Her courage throughout was an inspiration, perhaps even more so retrospectively, but it did not provide much solace. Aside from a child's death or severe and sudden handicap, I am hard pushed to imagine anything significantly worse than this for a parent. We withdrew into ourselves and our family unit. Nothing outside was relevant any longer and we must thank our friends who understood and stood by us from a discreet distance through these years of exclusion. Not all did.

Life is reduced to small incidents, many surprisingly trivial, but they all leave their mark, for ever. Nothing is as it was before, and it never will be. Imagine the father negotiating exactly how many drops of oil to put into a teaspoon as a salad dressing – no exaggeration. When weighing scales were 'allowed', the father's delight in 100 grams gained (how irrational for a scientist: of course I knew that this was within the range of uncertainty of the scales, but this did not diminish my delight or encouragement). And yes, manipulation is the obvious missing keyword from this story. We were lucky with Emily. She never lied, she was not usually in denial, when she said she wanted to get better and not continue to slip she meant it (really), but she was as manipulative as any other anorexic. Meals become ritual torture, for her I know, so much worse for her and I am not trying to compete with her suffering, but also for the parents. My ritual, this is a disease of rituals and obsession, was to say nothing. After all, Emily was being treated by experts and I knew that parents were so intimately intertwined with the disease that they were better in the background – this would have to get better one day and intervention would make things worse. Was I a coward or plain ignorant? Neither, I hope! I admit to capitulation and resignation on occasion, and this is not any better. I was drained, exhausted, used up. Rosane is so much more straightforward and direct. She simply could not sit through meals and witness her daughter's deliberate starvation, regardless of whose fault it was (or was not). Several times, she would suddenly jump up from table and shout that this could not go on, that a mother could not be a silent witness to her daughter's suicide. I wonder whether this helped. Perhaps it did. There would be a crisis; there would be tears but Emily would usually end up eating a little more that evening.

The tears and the eyes; oh the eyes. Sometimes choking, desperate, shaking, pathetic weeping (that awful sound) but more often, very often, simply tears. Large drops, extraordinary from that corpse, welling up from those unbearable eyes. The body withers, emaciated, haunting and haunted. The eyes do not change in colour: the same wonderful blue, but now in prominent orbits with no sparkle – never. That sparkle was replaced, for those years, by despair, dread, fear, utter sadness. Sometimes appealing for help and comfort that I could never provide, sometimes challenging and questioning, but blankly, without character, fathomless. Anorexia possesses the eyes too – the father sees and cannot forget.

The manipulation was itself quite fascinating, as indeed is anorexia as Emily pointed out herself in the early days. Emily had never manipulated any of us and is fundamentally a very straight, caring and sensitive person. But under Cruella's influence, her manipulative skills were truly bewitching. I happen to know a fair amount about metabolism, this comes with doing research in diabetes, but Emily outwitted me time and again. She had done her homework more diligently than this lazy biochemist!

Emily's experience with her psychiatrist did not surprise me – I have little patience with this area of clinical practice – but certainly shocked me and increased our desperation yet further. I do think that Dr D may have saved Emily's life, at the start, during the first critical months. But she, Dr D, was then so sterile and constantly negative, so coldly and (in my view) misguidedly professional, that she became Cruella's partner in crime (I do not use the word lightly). Clinical doctrine is not the solution to this disease. Treatment will only succeed if the professional, whoever that may be and regardless of his/her training and professional experience, understands what the patient is going through, understands the immense suffering and equally immense courage, and can combine this with stolid, obstinate, irresolute rules and discipline for a new life. Emily found these qualities in her heavenly twins, Louise and Vicki. The road to salvation was going to be a rough ride, and Emily's courage ultimately saved her life, but these two provided the roadmap and forced Emily to stick to it. Suddenly, it was going to be 'okay', to quote Louise's most famous expression.

There never was much reason for me to feel guilty. Emily

had convinced us that we were not to blame and I believe(d) her. I have read the scientific literature, for what it is worth, and have not found much to help me explain the aetiology or pathophysiology of this disease. Ironically, I have a natural tendency to feel guilty when even I can see I have no genuine reason to be so (a genetic, if not racial, trait). But when it came to the most important problem in my life, I could not feel guilty, strange as that may seem. I do, however, stand guilty as charged (by my wife, my mother, stepdaughter and Emily) of not showing or sharing my emotions, of not being affectionate enough (if only they knew what was going on inside). Perhaps implied or suggested affection and pride is not enough to nurture and comfort a growing girl – it surely is not. Did this help to destabilise Emily? Did this put her under pressure to succeed despite my intense (but too secret) pride and pleasure in seeing her already succeeding brilliantly in all she did? I fear so. So here is my guilt after all.

It is not over. The last few months have been hard; not nearly as bad as the worst months, but certainly a setback. Emily has lost weight again and we are back to playing games with food. But this is so different to the desperate, manipulative games of the early days. Emily is strong today and above all sparkles once again: she has plans, she laughs, she plays with her niece, she is dismissive about trivial issues that would have tormented her in the darkest months. She has written this book. She is alive. This is a temporary problem. It is part of 'growing out of anorexia' and this time I am not in denial or playing my own non-interventionist games. This too will be okay.

I love Emily.

There are a few keywords and phrases that come to mind when I think back over these past years and that may have helped me deal with Emily's anorexia. I hope that these may help other fathers in this situation but recognise that they may find no solace for their own predicament. This disease obviously has common symptoms, in addition to the most obvious loss of weight, but there are certainly features unique to each case and it would be simple minded to believe that there is a common solution and presumptuous to imagine that I could hold it. I use the example of a daughter because that is what I lived through. I have no idea how different this whole experience would have been had it been a son.

A father's instinct is right: if you think your daughter is behaving in an usual way or just seems 'out of sorts' for longer than in the past and you are alarmed, even slightly, then you should act on it. Do not talk yourself into complacency. It can happen to your own brilliant girl who has never caused you any trouble and who is to you and the world 'perfect'. She may not be so to herself but will surely not share this with you.

Talk! Communicate! But you should understand that the manipulation and deceit starts very early – do not be taken in: you know your child better than she does herself right now.

Your daughter is sick. There is nothing shameful about anorexia: no more so than diabetes or cancer. This is serious and it is not about to go away. Keep your head out of the sand without being alarmist. Do not let your daughter see your inner panic without being stoical. Fathers do not panic and mothers do not cry: we are the adults.

She needs professional help. You can help her greatly by asking around for advice. Who is the best person in your community? Can her school put you in contact with other families who might help? What about your GP? But never forget the specific sensitivity and responsiveness of each child: the professional you find must 'click' with your daughter. She is not 'another case'. She is special, as every anorexic girl is. Statistics are not helpful in the treatment of this or any other illness, but today's clinicians often forget this: there is no standard treatment. What works for one may be catastrophic for another (Dr D in Emily's story was greatly admired by one of her friends but detestable to Emily).

First your daughter may resist treatment. Next she might embrace it. Both reactions might be an artifice of her 'Cruella'. She may only willingly follow treatment from someone she feels 'understands her', perhaps meaning someone who will not push her beyond her comfort zone. She needs to be pushed but not tortured. The border is hard to find, the right person even harder. It is tough as a parent to step back and let someone else take over when your daughter comes home and says she is being hurt, that this is not working, that she promises she can do it alone, that you have to protect her.

The manipulation is relentless. There may also be lying (although we did not have this with Emily) – pathological lies and deceit. You will have to put up with it and understand that underneath it all, your daughter has not changed. She is fundamentally the same person and one day, maybe in months, maybe in a year or so, she will sparkle again. Until then, you must be resilient but without accepting all the deceit and without succumbing to the manipulation.

She may want to be comforted in quite surprising ways. The example of the 'lemon pie' episode with Dr D is revelatory in this regard (although I only discovered this years after the event. So much for communication!) When Emily came home and told us the story, we were deeply shocked and sympathised with Emily: such an awful experience, how could this supposed professional behave so callously, this is not the way forward, it is unacceptable to humiliate … Yet all Emily was asking was for us to tell her that eating the pie was okay so that she would feel less guilty!

The strain on the family will become unbearable. Your relationship with your wife and other children will be tested beyond normal limits. The bottom line is to trust each other and to never let the stress, the shock, the sadness, the frustration, the anger get the better of you. After a while the anorexia becomes all-consuming. I thought of little else during those critical months and years. Nothing else seemed important. But life does have to go on – in the office and at home. You cannot let it fall to pieces. Your daughter does not understand what you are going through but what she is suffering is worse – by an order of magnitude. She depends on you not just during the critical phase but will also need you, the family, the home, everything to be just like it was when she comes out of this, when she is really better.

Above all, it is not your fault. Maybe there was something you could have done better in the past, but you are not perfect either! There is no place for parental guilt or self-pity. Of course we can always do better and I think it important to try to use the illness to do so, so long as this is not in response to the manipulation. Make sure she knows that you have confidence in her and try to make her understand that her impression of having to do better and better, in everything, is a reflection of her illness and not of your expectations: she has over-achieved all her life and you know it. Can you make her believe it?

Yes, it is a rough ride, a roller coaster of a life. When you think it cannot get worse it does. When you think she is really over the hump, so much better, look at the smile, she went out with friends last night, there will be a setback. You will read and be told by 'friends' that anorexia is incurable. Perhaps so – it depends on one's definition of 'cure'. Your daughter will never be the same: Emily is not. So is there a cure if there have been these changes? In most respects the changes have strengthened her but the threat, the menace is still there. A change, a challenge, a death, a perceived failure, an uncertain future, could start the downward spiral again. Perhaps this fragility will disappear too one day and it will really be in the past – irrevocably. I would call that a cure, even if there are scars. You have to move forward. This is not easy and will never be so but you can help, as a father, to make it that little bit easier, for her, for your wife, for yourself. That's about all you can do but it is important. This will get better: she *will* get better.

From Amanda to sisters:

A few months ago, Emily sent the family an email asking us to write a passage to be included in this book. Our 'homework', as she called it, was to talk about our feelings and reactions to her anorexia and describe how we dealt with it. Both Emily's email and my reaction to it perhaps best describe the state our relationship had reached by the time Emily was writing her story.

I found Emily's email, arriving just a few months before the publication of her book, more demanding than she seemed to understand. I felt that Emily was wording her request in the comfort of the written rather than the spoken word. I felt that this had been something she had known about for a long time and should have discussed it with the family earlier. In fact, it turned out that I was the only one who was not aware of it and so I felt distanced once again. I also felt that writing a truthful account had deeper consequences for our relationship than Emily could foresee. She had discussed Cruella with our parents, Patrick and Sam on numerous occasions but we had stopped doing so in the last few years.

In recent years, Emily and I had become less close. My little baby sister retreated from me every time Cruella resurfaced. At the same time, instead of being the older sister I should have been, knocking on Emily's door and talking to her about my concern and love for her, I remained silent.

Since being asked to put my reaction to Cruella down in writing, I have been asking myself more than ever how two sisters who love each other and are concerned for one another could draw away from each other in times of difficulty. Was it because there is a gap of eleven years separating us? Was it because of our different personalities? Was it because I had my own worries with two small children and a marriage going through a rough time? Was it the fear of saying what I felt and hurting the family's and Emily's sensitive feelings in doing so? The answer probably lies in a combination of responses to all these questions as well as many others.

I left our home in Geneva to study at university in England when Emily was only seven years old. While at university I often returned home as the Oxford terms are relatively short. My little sister therefore remained my baby sister and our relationship remained a close one even with the eleven years separating us but it was perhaps more motherly than sisterly on my part. When I started working in London, however, and returned home less often, I missed most of Emily's adolescence and especially the beginnings of Cruella.

The summer Cruella was diagnosed as anorexia coincided with the planning of my wedding and my first months of pregnancy. This was a difficult time for us all and one during which both Emily and I needed our mother's attention. I can only begin to imagine how difficult it was for her, but it still hurts today to feel that my mother was not there emotionally for me on my special day and at a time when my hormones were flying high. Despite her suffering, Emily kept her optimism high during the preparations, which included food tastings (some at home), the pre-wedding dinner which was held at a restaurant serving only roasted chicken, potatoes, and a creamy desert (she came and she smiled) and the wedding day itself. Despite her frailty Emily, as thin and pale as she was in those days, got up in church in front of four hundred people and read the most touching text with a strong and cheeky voice. At dinner, Emily once again showed her courage and a read a beautiful poem that she had written herself to two hundred amazed guests and a teary-eyed sister. Cruella had not yet won; despite her appearance Emily was still Emily, my intelligent, creative, confident and cheeky sister (how I remember the cheeky hint in your voice when the text you read in church spoke of a wife's patience ...).

When Cecilia was born, Emily was again very present. She had asked me to hold on one more day from my due date as she needed to be there for the birth and magically I did! Emily was therefore with us on the night Cecilia decided to make her first appearance and I'll always keep in my head the image of Emily making toast with honey in our kitchen before going to hospital.

My memories of Cruella's onslaught become dimmer after the birth of Cecilia. Was I too busy and too involved in my own world as a new wife and mother? Did I not know how to react to Emily's deterioration and remained too cold as a result? Was I fed up having to tread on eggshells? Did I not want or was I too afraid to interfere when I did not agree with the way things were being done for Emily? Did I feel excluded from the trio that became Emily, my mother and Philippe and their endless, almost secret, discussions? Was this the time that Emily and I started digging that crevasse that distanced us so? The answer to these questions is yes, some emphatically, others less certain.

The other night, Emily and I went out for a heart-to-heart dinner, to have the discussion we both knew was well overdue. Although tense at first, we were able to talk and communicate and be honest with one another. We managed to feel that we were on the same wavelength and understand one another a little bit more. We could see that we could be the sisters we both wanted to be to each other. What happened at our dinner will remain private between Emily and me. However, I can say with confidence that these two sisters are closing a long disappointing chapter and are slowly turning to a new one which will be filled with honest words, more understanding and a love deeper than ever for one another.

It is difficult for me to give advice to other sisters as I do not feel that I was the most present sister for Emily in her most difficult times. So, the biggest piece of advice is *stay present*. Live your life, that is important, but be there for them, encourage and try to understand. If you don't, ask. If you still don't understand, then ask your parents: you are still a whole family. And as you are a whole family, do not hide your sadness, fears or anger: you are still another daughter and your parents are still your parents. Whatever happens, do not let distance settle in as it will be difficult and it will take time to repair, even once the anorexia is gone.

From Patrick to brothers:

Anorexia, my sister and me. Where to begin? When Emily asked me to write a chapter for her book, I was actually happy. I have been thinking about this disease and the impact it has been having on my sister and family so much for the last few years that I thought this would be something very easy to do. But as I sit here now I am not sure where to start. This has been such an emotional, confusing, hopeful and scary few years that it is hard to know how to discuss it.

I chose not to read Emily's book before writing this because I wanted to keep an open mind and not have my piece influenced by anything I might read. The truth is I am not sure what I can tell you that doesn't seem plainly obvious and that others haven't covered already in terms of the feelings one goes through when someone you love is affected by this terrible disease – and it really is terrible. So I want to write about one part of Emily's journey through anorexia where I was particularly close to her: when Emily got better.

In 2003, I moved to London from New York to start a new job. This was roughly at the same time that Emily had graduated from university and was moving to London too. As we were arriving at the same time, we decided to live together. I was quite apprehensive because I knew that I found it very difficult to be with Emily if she didn't eat but at the same time I was very much looking forward to it as I hadn't really been there for her regularly during her disease – now I was going to be able to be much more present for Emily.

As an aside, I do want to explain my relationship with Emily as I see it. Emily and I have always been very close and I have always been extremely fond and protective of my little sister. However, since I left home when Emily was only thirteen, I did not have a daily relationship with her during some of the most important years of her life – and when she fell ill. I only spoke to Emily on the phone every now and then and saw her on family holidays or when she and the family were visiting me wherever I was.

When I would come home and see Emily ill (I couldn't bear to look at her so skinny and starving herself at times),

I would find it very difficult not to say anything. My family seemed to have this way of tip-toeing around her as all they wanted was to make everything easy for her so that at meal-times she would eat *something* – anything. These meals were difficult and though we all tried to pretend we were having a normal, family time, we were all looking at Emily's plate. Emily knew this and it drove her crazy to have all the attention secretly focused on her, but I think she also hated it because she knew it meant she had to eat. I hated it because I could not stand to keep quiet and let Emily do this to herself, and I also could not continue to see her control the whole family's eating habits.

After a few days of me being back home and experiencing what my poor parents had to live through on a daily basis, I would feel I had to confront her. I couldn't remain silent and watch my little sister effectively commit herself to a slow death through starvation. Emily would sense my frustration growing and she would usually try to avoid me as she knew I would approach her and push her to face her disease and herself. Emily was very good at manipulating our emotions and making us feel guilty for confronting her but I think it was easier for me as I had the benefit of not being home all the time. So the moment would come when I would inevitably confront her and everything would come out. These were always lengthy, intense discussions with a lot of tears and plenty of emotion, but we would end by trying to find ways of making things better for her. I think these talks were for the most part honest and helpful, and allowed Emily and me to stay close to each other and for me to better understand what she was going through.

So I remained close to Emily and the situation in the way I knew best: by talking. Emily would call me in her moments of crisis and I would always take the time to speak to her, counsel her and help her however I could. I felt so far away and helpless when I received these phone calls. I have also always expressed my feelings to her so I never really kept things bottled up inside and Emily knew more or less how I was feeling through all of this too.

Back to Emily and me moving in together. I was excited because this was a chance to get to know my little sister better and to try to also have a normal relationship with her, outside of her disease. I was, however, really scared that her eating habits would be unbearable and that she would inadvertently control my eating habits as well. I had seen her do this to my parents and I was determined not to let her do this to me. I remember coming home to Geneva one day, when Emily was at home, and my mother telling me lunch or dinner was ready and when I came down and only saw salad and steamed vegetables, I went crazy. I told my mother this was not a meal, that we needed bread, and meat, and I didn't care how sick my sister was, *we* had to eat normally. I still feel bad about this because I can't begin to imagine how difficult it was for my parents who had to have meals with Emily every day – they were only doing their best to make sure Emily was eating whatever she could.

In the end though, living with Emily was very easy. We didn't fight (not even normal brother/sister stuff) and I didn't have to use different pots/pans/brushes, etc., for my greasy foods. Of course there was some control over the kitchen and Emily did have to have her 'own' foods, and meals at set times but nothing as bad as what I had feared. Sam was there regularly and would cook some of his amazing meals (with olive and other oils) and Emily would even eat what he cooked with us. I was lucky. It turns out I lived with Emily at a time when she was doing well and was ... back to normal?

I look back on this time and think of a lot of things. Of course I was highly analytical of Emily and watched everything to see how she was doing, but after a while I felt there was not so much for me to be worried about. She was really eating quite normally and large meals. We also went out to restaurants a few times and the choice of restaurant was easy (restaurants had been so difficult in the past). Emily, would say 'we can go anywhere, don't worry I'll find something on the menu I can eat' – a *huge* step! She was eating normally, she had put on weight and was looking healthy and happy – she even got her period back at one point, which I understood meant she was reaching the right weight for her body and was giving it all the foods it needed.

So my very sick little sister was becoming not so sick any more? Not quite. But she was better and I think we all made a few mistakes in terms of how we dealt with it then and now. First of all Emily put on weight. She was looking normal and healthy but she felt fat. She looked for reassurance in everybody and we told her it was normal that she was a little 'puffy' because she was putting things into her diet that her body was not used to any more so she was reacting this way. It would pass. She was, however, neither 'fat' nor 'puffy': she was healthy. Her body was the way it should be and the proof was in the fact that she had enough body fat to be able (briefly) to have her period again. Of course she looked bigger – we hadn't seen Emily with an ounce of fat on her body in four years. We reassured her though and she then went and did some ridiculous nutritional test that resulted in her finding out that she was 'intolerant' to just about every food (or so it seemed to me). So she started cutting things out of her diet again – religiously.

Back to control. We had been so close. Emily had been able to eat just about everything and even seemed to enjoy things she had deprived herself of for so long but now she was controlling again. We let it be because she had done a

309

'scientific' test that showed she was 'intolerant' to various foods so, of course, if she was 'intolerant', she shouldn't eat them. This, in my mind, set Emily back. We should have told Emily she looked fine, not because it was the right thing to say but because it was true. Emily had been at a place where this disease did not control her whole life, where her body was functioning normally and we humoured her when she said she felt fat. How could we?

Second, I think we made the mistake of looking at Emily when she became well again in saying 'at least she is not as bad as she was'. Of course this was true but we are all forgetting that it was also not as good as it had been. We have too often been too quick to look for success when this disease is not having a disastrous effect on Emily when we should really be remembering the Emily that can be as good as she was.

Anorexia as we witnessed it has been such a roller coaster of a ride and has taken so many different shapes with Emily. Emily has unbelievable eyes – when she is well, they look amazing. Her eyes speak so much about what is going on inside and so many times I have found it so difficult to look into them and catch a glimpse of the torture taking control of Emily.

Emily says she is getting there and I have decided it is time to give her the benefit of the doubt; to let her take charge of her own destiny. Much about this disease is about learning to let go. Emily has to learn to let go and not be so controlling all the time. We, as her family, have to let go and let her grow up on her own for once. We have all been too protective, too controlling of her – we too need to let go now. We have given her all the tools and support she needs and we will continue to do so. However, if Emily is going to have a normal relationship with food and herself for good, and stop doing irreparable harm to her body once and for all, only she can do it. I believe she will do it. I have faith in my little sister. I always have.

So how did I feel going through all of this? There was a mixture of emotions. Most of them close to concern and fear. I felt helpless but never hopeless. I always thought there was a solution and continue to think this today. For me this whole ordeal has always been about getting Emily better. I never dwelled (or dwell) on my own feelings for too long because I am not bothered by them. I don't find sadness/concern/fear that difficult to deal with – I just look for ways to fix the problem that brings these emotions on. That is the person I am so my approach to Emily's anorexia has always been to be able to be there for *her* when *she* needed me and to try and find a way out for *her*. I couldn't go on writing for ever about my feelings, not because I don't want to but because that is not my experience with this disease. My experience has always been to be pragmatic and look for solutions. I don't want to trivialise this disease by saying this – anorexia is a highly complex and destructive disorder but it is treatable.

What advice can I give to brothers who go through this? Stay positive. Learn about this disease (when you start to talk to others about it, you quickly find that many have experiences with anorexia that you can learn from). Communicate – this is crucial in my mind. Keep lines of communication open with everybody in the family and especially 'your Emily'. Don't ignore symptoms – say something if you think something is wrong. Don't feel responsible – this is not your fault. Be there for your parents too – this is very tough on them and they will inevitably feel responsible. Speak to your sister's friends and boyfriend and hear what they have to say. I think we may have excluded some friends from our family who shared this too and we should have perhaps spoken to them more. Continue to live your life. Be very present, involved and help as much as you possibly can but come to terms with the fact that at the end of the day, the only person that can really fix this is the one suffering. All you can do is help and you should.

From Olivia to best friends:

Emily is my best friend.

Emily whom I have known since I was ten years old, with whom I spent all my weekends and holidays from then on:

Emily my soul mate. A soul mate who at fifteen was slowly turning into someone I no longer knew or understood.

When Emily asked me to write, I couldn't remember anything: neither words nor feelings – I had blanked out a whole period of my life; I was numb. Why? Some told me I was trying to protect myself, while others suggested that (at the time) I was just too young to understand what was really happening. The truth is I was quite quick to notice that something was wrong. However, for a very long time Emily and I just did not talk about it. I think we probably did not fully acknowledge the extent or depth of the problem. At the time, I thought she was just a 'normal' fifteen-year-old girl who wanted to look good, fresh and healthy for an upcoming school fashion show in which she was going to take part. I wasn't really worried as Emily had always been 'healthily health conscious'; she would work-out, eat healthily and, if I had any doubts, the occasional midnight feast managed to reassure me.

The only thing that did start worrying me was Emily's constant quest for perfection. She has and always will be a perfectionist; however, recently, she had started pushing her perfectionism to the limits and applied it to everything she would do – even at fifteen, one realises that perfectionism is one thing, excessiveness another.

The first-ever fight Emily and I had took place during a holiday we took to Santo Domingo, one month before the infamous fashion show. We were together with my mother – who frequently questioned me on Emily's health suggesting she might suffer from anorexia. I defended Emily: Emily is fine, she just wants to look her best for the summer, she's had a very hectic academic year, we've just done sixty laps in the pool AND we're both a bit consti-pated so even though it's lunch time Emily wants to have a really LIGHT lunch. And she isn't vomiting so she can't be anorexic. Any excuse was good. I wasn't really refusing to face the facts but it just couldn't be true: Emily was not ill. She did seem a bit pale and run down these days but maybe she was just tired? I couldn't help but wonder: why is everyone so worried? She is okay, maybe not 100 per cent but if she really wasn't well I certainly think I'd be the first to know! Food shopping became a bit of a nightmare and I would get annoyed and irritated by her behaviour. Okay, we can have carrots (Emily was thin but then again the amount of beta carotene we were getting from the carrots gave us a fabulous tan!) and green beans (again) but let's have some avocado as well? I would put the avocado in the trolley and she would put it back on the shelf. She didn't tolerate any fat at all; she wanted to be in total control of the food she was eating. Over the course of that holiday, Emily changed and became a stranger to me. She had not only become increasingly defensive and aggressive but mostly frighten-ingly competitive. She was constantly challenging me, whether during our meals or in the swimming pool, who would eat less or who could do the most laps as if she was trying to prove that she had control over everything. Her competitiveness was like her perfectionism: everything had to be done and dealt with in an excessive way.

At this point, what scared me most about Emily's behaviour was the implicitness of her actions. I did not understand why she couldn't just simply tell me things, talk to me. Did she not trust me? Did she herself not really know what was happening? Instead, she was unconsciously and silently forcing me to comply and obey her rules. By the end of the holiday, even I had now become slightly competitive and things had really changed between us. Emily had 'gone'; my sister, best friend and soul mate had become someone I no longer recognised or knew. I was worried, frightened and extremely angry with her. Did she honestly think that we would manage to remain best friends if we weren't even on the same wavelength any more? After everything I had done for her, didn't she have any consideration whatsoever for me and my feelings? How could she be so selfish as to wander off to another world without even consulting me?

Nonetheless, I put my teenage feelings to one side: Emily was suffering and needed support. I knew I wasn't going to be able to follow her all the way and cope for ever but I decided to help her as much as I could.

It wasn't a teen body obsession any more: that summer she was diagnosed with anorexia.

For over a year, I had lunch with Emily at our school canteen every single day and even though I wasn't 100 per cent aware of the problem, I strongly sensed something was wrong. She was stressed out, refused to eat with anyone else and was becoming increasingly dependent on me. On a 'good' day, Emily would add rice to her plate of crudités/vegetables drowned in balsamic vinegar; on a 'bad' day, rice would not be on the menu. I cannot remember if rice simply wasn't on the school menu that day or if it just wasn't on Emily's (menu). What I can definitely remember is that the occasional bad day turned into a bad week and then into a bad month. After a while there were no more good days, just bad ones. Emily's definition of good and bad, right and wrong, was now influenced by the fluctuations in her weight. In effect, in her new world a bad day meant anything remotely dipped in oil (not to mention butter), a good day meant vegetables: pure, dry, watery, steamed, raw; tasteless greens. Her food intake was now going to be dictated by some rules she had set up regarding how much food she was allowed and how much exercise would be needed after eating certain quantities and types of food.

I think the people around us recognised there was a problem and noticed that a certain pattern-routine was developing. By the middle of that academic year (our final year) classmates would find any excuse to come up to us during our lunch in order to (I am sure) check what was on our plates. After a while, I began feeling psychologically fragile: the constant staring and whispering around us was becoming difficult to handle. I refused to talk about this with Emily: she had enough to deal with these days. Did she need to know things were beginning to affect me? But she seemed too immersed in her new, her very own calorie-and-fat-free world these days to worry about the gossiping. As a matter of fact, I wonder whether she ever did notice the constant glaring, staring and whispering.

'Till Oxford and beyond' had always been our motto; my friendship and help would also last till then, but not beyond. We had always wanted to study in Oxford. We managed to do so and even shared a flat for a year. A year that I now consider as the most painful and disturbing year of my life. In theory it could have been perfect but Emily had been ill for a few years now, and even though she had ups and downs, I couldn't see any true amelioration of her condition. She would never really discuss her weight/health issues with me and I must admit I never really dared to ask. So I had no real psychological insight: I could only tell by her physical status. Had she put on a few kilos or lost a few? Was her skin paler, lips cracked, was she cold, did her neck look longer, her hands skinnier? From assessing her to checking the bins to see how many vegetables she had or hadn't eaten, I found myself constantly inspecting and verifying everything in order to evaluate the situation, know where to stand and how to react.

Her health was deteriorating, my nerves were growing more and more fragile by the minute, and for the very first time I somehow started to lose interest in her. How could anyone ever become so thin? She looked terrible. I felt disgusted and sometimes found myself on the verge of a nervous breakdown. I wanted to yell at her, insult her, hit her. I wanted her to wake up and take a grip of herself. Her behaviour was increasingly compulsive: everything was problematic, from the washing up (we each had our own sponge as she refused to share the same sponge in case it came in contact with residues of 'inedible' foods such as fat or sugar) to the space reserved for her food in the fridge. Everything had become systematic, there was a rule for everything. She was disgusted by everything … I was living in a freak world.

The relationship was becoming more and more unhealthy. I couldn't confront her at all, often finding it difficult to discuss the weather with her. She would say, 'Olive, tell me if there's something wrong.' How could I possibly tell her she looked like a soulless and lifeless skeleton? At the time, I assumed any confrontation would make her lose another few grams, grams she simply couldn't afford to shed off. That year, I really thought she was going to die. She was losing too much weight. I was incapable of really doing anything; I was just witnessing this life-threatening illness. She was also developing some kind of schizophrenic behaviour. She would react, over-react and then apologise by sending me letters that she would place on my bed when I was gone, slide under my door or leave on my plate before dinner. Everything I would do was wrong and she was always right. It had become unbearable, frightening. I felt distressed.

From the very beginning when she asked me to live with her, I knew I was making a mistake. Her illness had crept up on her again and I knew I wouldn't be able to help her any longer but something forced me to do it. Strangely enough I felt like I owed her something. A few people tried to discourage me but once again I refused to listen. My parents were worried I wouldn't be able to cope and they were right. I still do not know if that year really separated us or if the distancing was due to an accumulation of things we had been through over the years. In spite of our friendship and the love and affection I had for her, my natural instincts told me it was time to protect myself. It had all been too intensive, too scary – simply too much.

Remains of our friendship lie in the past. We scrape together what we can at present and perhaps will further piece the puzzle back to whole in future. In some ways I am sure our friendship will last to that 'beyond' of which we always spoke; however, I cannot pretend that things are the same, she and I both know that, and I don't know whether they ever will be, really, again.

Do I have any regrets? Not really. But yes, I sometimes wish I had had the guts and strength to confront her; not to tread on eggshells, constantly. I wish I had told her when she pissed me off for refusing to eat even half a (table) spoonful of the couscous I had prepared, or had suggested that she pile fewer vegetables (there were SO many) on her plate for dinner and add something a little more consistent instead.

It has been a roller coaster ride for us all, but as far as I am concerned I must admit that the situation very often left me breathless.

From Sam to boyfriends:

I remember the email Emily wrote me from Geneva when she spent the term there. *I'm anorexic* (although in many more words). We were friends – good friends but not as close as we would soon become and there were no romantic twinkles as yet – so the deluge of words and feelings (the first of many) was slightly unexpected and un-English! I didn't quite know how to react. Then she came back to

Oxford; a group of us went out to lunch and she had a pizza, so I thought that probably meant she was okay again. Little had I realised that the pizza was 'cheese-free' (perhaps even oil-free?); covered solely in tomato chunks and a sprinkle of oregano for added taste.

I cannot overstate my ignorance of the disease before I met Emily. Having been for a pizza, surely it was all okay, we could now move on. So we went for a curry – because Emily had always had this obsession with oriental flavours, spices and smells, but had never been for that most British and student ritual, 'going for an Indian'. When her vegetable curry arrived, and looked a bit greasy, I can *now* imagine what went through her head, but at the time it didn't cross my mind. I showed off my knowledge of Indian cooking by describing the use of ghee – clarified butter. The gist of my story was that the butter was heated so that all the milk solids (*the goodness*) floated the top and were skimmed off, leaving pure, 100 per cent *fat*. I remember the look on her face as she had a few more brave mouthfuls, and she has now shown me her diary entry for that day. The impact of my ill-judged words and the image of ultimate evil that they inspired in her was lost on me at the time, and I am still ashamed of my insensitivity.

I would learn fast as her boyfriend. I think I was in love with her before I finally asked her out on a damp autumnal evening in November 2002. I fell in love with the eyes and their sparkle, the fact that she was unique, beautiful, cheeky, 'Swiss Miss'. We had been on the 'road trip' that summer, driving around France and Italy – the 'final stage' of Emily's recovery from the first Oxford episode and a time when she let go and laughed again. There have been many of these false summits since.

When I see photos of Emily at 'ground zero', or think about that period in the summer of 2003, it makes me feel nauseous. My beautiful girlfriend had gone AWOL. Tracksuits replaced jeans as jeans fell off, big woolly jumpers replaced little tops, straggly hair replaced the continental gloss of good health and careful maintenance, the electric blue eyes grew to vacuous grey saucers in a bony, colourless face, translucent skin pulled tight at the temple and jaws.

The overwhelming feeling at the time was one of helplessness. The girl I loved was starving herself in front of me and there was nothing I could do to make it better. We would have conversations that tracked the logic of the situation: you are too thin, you are dangerously thin, you are doing permanent damage to your body, you acknowledge this, and to stop this you have to eat more. Olive oil is good for you, your body needs 'healthy' oils to function optimally.

I know I know I know I know, answered Emily, but she could not act upon her words.

The concept of 'Cruella' – the demonic possession of Emily by a force of profound evil, a twister of image and logic – has stuck because it is the most accurate reflection of the disease. It is also a way that those who love the 'possessed' can differentiate between the girl and the disease. Together victim and allies can unite against a common enemy, and their anger is aimed at a common target. Cruella had consumed the girl with whom I had fallen in love – she had stolen her smile, her laugh, her twinkle, her fun.

There were times when I was desperate for a normal relationship with a 'normal' girl, one who didn't lock herself up at night in a big woolly jumper with a giant mug of herbal tea just to stay warm. There were times when I snapped, lost patience, shouted. These moments were followed by the inevitable tears, apologies, vows to get better, and sometimes a letter pouring out words that did not flow so easily in speech. I felt frustrated and angry – frustrated because the steps towards recovery were small and erratic; that I could do nothing about it, nor, it seemed, could any doctor; that I could never, as a man with a near-romantic love of food, understand how anyone could not want to eat and angry because sometimes the end seemed to be so far away. I remember at one point I spoke to a friend's sister who had been through something similar – she told me to be patient and that one day Emily would sit down and have a hot chocolate (with skimmed milk). At the time the thought of this seemed ridiculous; now it seems achievable.

The physical effect of the disease was, and is, terrifying, but the way it chokes a personality is the most upsetting. Emily became controlling to a psychopathic degree. The world outside was dirty and full of 'microbes' that had to be washed away before going to bed; there were separate scrubbing brushes for Emily's mugs, plates, her saucepans and my saucepans; no one could sit on her bed because of the contamination risk of 'filth' – there were dozens more that I have – thankfully – forgotten. The tears came almost every day – sometimes for no discernible reason, sometimes after an argument, out of exhaustion. She was snappy, cold, distant, desperate. Most of our friends would ask me how she was doing instead of asking her – she was almost unrecognisable, physically and behaviourally, and people were scared of what reaction they would get were they to ask directly.

The reason that this seemingly untenable relationship lasted through that period is that Emily never lied to me or her family about the situation. She was not in denial of the problem: she could always talk about it, articulate her feelings to the nth degree, and although this sometimes added to the frustration, at least lines of communication remained open and trust intact.

Fundamentally the story has a happy ending, albeit with

caveats. *My* Emily – the girl I fell in love with – is back; Cruella is exiled and must be fought off when she threatens to return. She returned recently for a brief visit, and the troops were rallied – Emily is seeing Vicki and Louise again and I trust them to give her the psycho-nutritional support she needs that I cannot give. But like a smell that takes you back to a memory more vividly than a picture, so too does the mention of those names take me back to 'ground zero'.

This time will be the final push. I am positive, hopeful. I have watched Emily writing this book and unloading every detail of this struggle. I have seen its therapeutic effect – another stage of healing. Our relationship is stronger than it has ever been. I have learned to be independent, not to be afraid to do my own thing, to stand up to the occasional tantrum, to establish boundaries so that boyfriend remains just that and neither therapist nor nutritionist (although I am still her 'favourite chef'!).

Despite Emily's permanent fear that I will suddenly, one day, unleash two years of pent-up rage and frustration, those feelings are dissolved. In the nearly five years we have been together, I have seen a girl destroyed and repaired, rebuilt. I feel hope and relief, and when I see her eyes alive again, and the cheeky smile, I know it was all worth it.

A boyfriend, unlike a family, has the option of walking away. I am glad I did not. I came close to being pushed away, partly through Emily's extreme guilt that she could not be the girlfriend she wanted to be, and partly because of the sheer difficulty of being around a person in her state. The most important thing is *patience* – recovery will come with the right support network and encouragement (bullying and threats are counter-productive) and to remember that the person who snaps, cries, freezes you out is not the person you love, but a parasitical disease in control of her.

Share the burden. You cannot go through this by yourself and need to involve family, friends and professionals in the process as far as possible. To maintain any semblance of normality in the relationship you cannot be both shrink and boyfriend at the same time. You are the boyfriend.

Encourage and praise instead of cajoling and putting down. As this is a disease that preys on guilt: to be disappointed or angry when the victim loses weight, trips up, slips back is to feed this monster. To encourage and remain positive is exhausting but constructive – finding approval, inspiring pride, seeing perspective and being loved are the most powerful antidotes to the illness and you can help to administer them. You, in turn, need to be supported by friends and maintain your identity and life beyond the reach of 'Cruella'.

Perfect

Above all you need hope, patience, persistence and perspective to remind yourself this will pass, your Emily will return, you will be happy again.

The worst is behind, my Emily is back, and I, she, we are happy.

Postscript

20 August 2008

I always swore never to harbour any regrets. I swore never more to be stifled by repentance. And that the unavoidable whisper of remorse would be hushed in the writing of this book.

Yet when I handed in my manuscript it was with *regret*. Because, by then, She had managed to creep in on me once again, armed with the intent of thwarting my message of hope. And I had let her.

Which is why I was so eager for a chance to write just a few lines more. Because now, a year on, I can finally bring this story to a happy close.

Last month, on 12 July, Sam asked me to marry him. And I said 'yes' – well, actually, 'Are you sure??' and then 'Yes!' It was under the moon, overlooking the sea; he got down on one knee, and I began to tremble. The sort of thing you read about in books . . .

Then last week, after more than five years of 'nothingness', and the worry that this time I really had caused my body irreparable damage, the moon did wink again, and that clock did wind itself back to a fertile tick!

Today I can say, with confidence, that while I will never forget Cruella and the all too central part she played through eight important years of my life, I have managed to let her go, for good.

I no longer fall asleep to the sum of my daily meals; I no longer wake up to the calculation of what food is yet to come. I am free to care for those I love; my hands are free to reach out to others. I am free to go fetch my dreams, to laugh, to giggle a cheeky chuckle, to act like a child if I want to, but above all to grow up, and I look forward to discovering what the future holds, ready to face whatever it throws my way; *our* way.

With these final words I am at present freed of my one aching regret, and I have ultimately proven Her wrong: there really *is* hope, and fairy tales really *can* come true.

So there you have it, my 'Perfect' ending!

Em xx

This is the story of a little girl who
Was good, and kind, and well-behaved – just like you

She lived in a pretty house at the end of a sunny street all
    beautifully lined with trees
Where birds would twitter and squirrels would chatter
    and butterflies would dance with the bees

This little girl loved to skip her way to school and hop all
    the way home up the stairs
Where she would play with her toys and make lots of noise
    and then she would cuddle her bears

At school she learned all sorts of clever things – though she
    found mathematics quite a bore
And when the bell rang at the end of the day she always
    wanted to stay and learn more

She had lots of friends – too many to name. They had
    sleepovers and giggled in the dark
They had fun dressing up, sharing stories, baking cakes;
    making grass stains running wild in the park

She was kind, she was thoughtful, she always wanted to
    please, to make people happy and glad
She was loved, she was lucky, she had everything a girl
    could need and was grateful for all that she had

Her Christmas wish list always started with peace on
earth, end of war and health all around
She wanted dolphins to be saved and criminals to behave
and for stray puppy dogs a home to be found

And whenever she saw two people fight in the street she
would always stop to ask why
Then get them to make up, shake hands, sometimes hug
and wave a friendly good-bye

In trains and buses when everyone was squished, rudely
treading on each other's feet
She would spot a tired old lady, wave for her to come and
stand up to offer her a seat

This little girl dreamed of growing up and all the
amazing things that she would do
When she was an adult and went to university and maybe
even drove her own car too!

Soon that day came when she had finished school and it
now was time for her to leave
To pack up her clothes and put on a brave face for all
those great things she wanted to achieve

But one morning she woke up and suddenly was afraid,
not so sure that she was quite good enough
It was a very big world and she was only just a girl; yes
the whole thing felt altogether too tough

Perfect

Next she looked in a mirror and hated what she saw; she
  felt ugly and wanted to hide
Everything about her was ordinary and dull; nobody could
  ever want her by their side

She wanted so much to do well, to be great; she wanted to
  do her very best
Yet she searched everywhere and still could not find those
  talents with which she had been blessed

This little girl stopped eating one day, because it was all
  too much, too much, too much
It felt like she was walking up a very steep hill with two
  broken legs and no crutch

'Like this it feels safe,' she kept telling herself, 'this way I
  don't have to grow old'
So she shrivelled and shrank and looked pale and blank —
  and shivered all day long from the cold

Everyone was worried and wondered what to do; if only
  they could get her to see
That the beautiful girl she always had been, she still was
  and always would be

But she couldn't believe anything they said was true, she
  knew they were lying because
Whenever she took out her mirror to check, she still hated
  the person she was

This little girl became very ill and needed a helping hand
Someone who could talk to her, rescue her, set her free: get
her finally to understand

That she needn't be afraid of the big world out there; that
it all was going to be okay
She must believe in herself and keep her head high, then
she would be fine come what may

She must know there was only one thing anyone wanted
from her and that was for her to smile
If she could live her life fully and make the most of every
day, then it would all be worthwhile

She needn't be 'perfect', nor always the best, and sometimes
she might even get things wrong
But she would pick herself up and learn from her mistakes
and that was how she would get strong

So this little girl chose to give it a go; she took a giant
jump and what do you know?
First a spoonful of peas then a little more if you please and
soon she was starting to grow!

And she wasn't scared anymore as she now could be sure
that what really counts above all
Is the love you receive and the love that you give; it is love
that will catch any fall.

Bibliography

A few memorable books that offered me some light:

Edelman, Sarah, *Change Your Thinking: Overcome Stress, Combat Anxiety and Improve Your Life with CBT*, Vermilion, London, 2006

Edgson, Vicki, and Dr Wendy Denning, *The Diet Doctors: Inside and Out*, Vermilion, London, 2006

Edgson, Vicki, and Ian Marber, *The Food Doctor: Healing Foods for Mind and Body*, Collins & Brown, London, 2004

Greive, Bradley Trevor, *Tomorrow: Adventures in an Uncertain World*, Andrews McMeel Publishing, Kansas City, 2003

Hoff, Benjamin, *The Tao of Pooh and Te of Piglet*, Methuen Young Books, London, 2002

Jeffers, Susan, *Feel the Fear and Do it Anyway*, Arrow Books, London, 1991

The Moosewood Collective, *Moosewood Restaurant Cookbook*, Ten Speed Press, Berkeley, 1985

Orbach, Susie, *On Eating*, Penguin, London, 2002

There are so many more great titles out there. I highly recommend that you go find your own.

About the Author

Emily Halban was born in Geneva in 1983 and spent her childhood there before moving to England to study at Oxford University. Emily developed anorexia at the age of sixteen and suffered from the disease for eight years, sitting Oxford finals in a separate room so she could be continuously fed throughout. She graduated in 2004 and moved to London where she now leads a healthy life with her fiancé, Sam.